NIC FRANCES MBE is a world-renowned social entrepreneur. In 2007 he started a for-profit environmental and social purpose enterprise called Cool **nrg** working to drive environmental change globally. Nic first worked in the corporate world of hospitality as well as stockbroking. He was later instrumental in establishing two UK social businesses and received an MBE from the British Government for services to charity before coming to Australia to become CEO of The Brotherhood of St Laurence. From 2004–2007 he founded and led Easy Being Green. Nic has been recognised as a Schwab Foundation social entrepreneur and attends the World Economic Forum in this capacity. In 1996 he was ordained as an Anglican priest.

THE END OF CHARITY

TIME FOR SOCIAL ENTERPRISE

NIC FRANCES
WITH MARYROSE CUSKELLY

ALLEN&UNWIN

First published in 2008

Copyright © Nic Frances 2008

Allen & Unwin
83 Alexander Street
Crows Nest NSW 2065
Australia
Phone: (61 2) 8425 0100
Fax: (61 2) 9906 2218
Email: info@allenandunwin.com
Web: www.allenandunwin.com

National Library of Australia
Cataloguing-in-Publication entry:

Frances, Nic.

The end of charity : time for social enterprise / authors,
Nic Frances ; Maryrose Cuskelly.

978 1 74175 263 2 (pbk.)
Includes index.

Sustainable development; Social services, Charities, Human services

Cuskelly, Maryrose.

338.9

Set in 12/14 pt Minion by Midland Typesetters, Australia
Printed and bound in Australia by Griffin Press

10 9 8 7 6 5 4 3 2 1

The pages of this book are printed on 100% ancient-forest friendly paper.

The paper this book is printed on is certified by the © 1996 Forest Stewardship Council A.C. (FSC). The printer holds FSC chain of custody SCS-COC-001185. The FSC promotes environmentally responsible, socially beneficial and economically viable management of the world's forests.

FSC
Mixed Sources
Product group from well-managed forests and other controlled sources
Cert no. SCS-COC-001185
www.fsc.org
© 1996 Forest Stewardship Council

Contents

Acknowledgements

We would like to acknowledge the generous contributions of Peter Botsman, Dr Pamela Hartigan, Jackie Yowell, Helen Grasswill, John Elkington, Marc Benioff, Mirai Chatterjee, Phillip Cohn, Paulo Coelho, Hilde Schwab, Evan Thornley, Peter Thomson, Gerhardt Pearson and Jeremy Gilley.

Maryrose and Nic

Thanks to all those in Liverpool who were there at the start of the journey. I would also like to express my gratitude to the Schwab Foundation, the World Economic Forum and Klaus and Hilde Schwab for their support and for providing the space to have the conversations that have challenged me and my ideas. This has been instrumental in developing the ideas I have expressed in this book. I hope to go on being challenged, and to continue challenging others.

On a personal note, much of the learning reflected in this book was made while I was married to Philippa. Although we are no longer together, I wish to thank her as much as anyone for her support on my journey and for being the mother of our two beautiful children, Holly and Charlie.

And really, at the heart of good business is service and a deal, Danny and Dad, thank you for all the lessons.

To Charlie and Holly, it is my love for you that fills me up and keeps me focused on doing the best I can for our world.

Lastly, I have tried to write this book a dozen times; it's written because of Maryrose's gracious skill and commitment. Thank you, Maryrose.

Nic

1

The case for change

This book aims to engender a new dialogue: a dialogue about creating the conditions under which business, government, the welfare sector and individuals can address the problems of poverty, inequality and environmental sustainability. In order to grapple with these issues effectively we as a society must reclaim the word value as a term that reflects what we hold as desirable and important—the things and ideas for which we choose to strive. We need to move beyond notions of charity and welfare, beyond do-gooding and guilt, to a system that recognises the complexity of our values and a realistic understanding of how we can support them. The way to do this, I believe, is to embrace what I have come to call value-centred market economics.

In recent times, we have become increasingly focused on valuing things in terms of money alone. Yet money is merely the mechanism we have chosen as a means to share and exchange things of value. In itself—without the objects, services or opportunities that it creates—money is worthless.

Paradoxically, while we refuse to acknowledge value in anything other than monetary terms, there are some things that loom like the proverbial elephant in the room of the economy, uncosted and unvalued. These things include poverty, homelessness, disadvantage, climate change, water management and other environmental realities. By turning a blind eye to the very real market value/cost of these things, we subsidise and tolerate inefficiency, environmental damage and social inequality. To confront these problems and devise long-term, large-scale solutions, products and their by-products must be ascribed their true value.

There is no need to fear that the changes flowing from such a rethink will slow economic activity or reduce opportunities for enterprise; as markets shift they generate new economic value. Yes, some industries and individual companies will face shrinking markets and increased costs as their products are ascribed their true value/cost. However, other markets will be created and extended. For example, in recent years, in a bid to check global warming, carbon has been ascribed a value. This has created huge new markets for products such as compact fluorescent light bulbs. Similarly, the demand for 4WD vehicles may shrink as oil prices increase, but consumer interest in more fuel-efficient cars is rising.

These types of market shifts resulting from changes in values are not unprecedented. Over the last few decades, the tobacco industry has had to come to terms with the true cost of its product. As a result of increased awareness of tobacco's adverse effect on health, cigarette companies have had to take some responsibility for the costs its use generates for society as a whole. Through litigation, government regulation and increased taxes on their product, they have been forced, in some measure, to subsidise the huge costs to our health system and compensate those whose lives have been shortened by smoking.

New opportunities and new markets have always emerged in response to shifting values, and these value shifts can be supported by legislation or other market mechanisms. In fact, the market itself is one of the most powerful tools we have to deliver and effect social change on a large scale and support the values we want our society to advocate.

Our political and economic system divorces values from the market. Historically, those on the left have focused on social values, while conservatives have made the management of the economy and the market their province. The welfare sector, of which for many years I was a part—most recently, as CEO of the Brotherhood of St Laurence—also operates within this system, as do business and enterprise. Although each of these elements is part of the one system, they operate in their own cycles of separateness.

With each element focusing on its particular area of concern, problems for and disjunctions with the other elements and sectors are created. Each sector also draws its meaning and status in part from its differences, both real and perceived, from the other sectors. The system is set up to fail—has to have its failings—in order for each sector to know its place: as CEO of a large welfare agency, I needed homeless people to define myself as a 'good' person in contrast to those in the less 'caring' sectors of business and government.

Individuals and entities within each sector define themselves and draw their raison d'être from the place where they've chosen to reside: I'm in business, I make money; I'm in charity, I do good works. Such separation allows individuals to restrict their engagement with the world to manageable dimensions. This keeps their sphere of action and engagement a straightforward place to reside in, if a little uncomfortable to maintain. Decision making within this restricted world view is also much simpler. The consequence of such separation is that we can't bring all the available levers to bear on any particular problem.

Faced with a problem, the tendency has been for each sector to take a different and usually disconnected approach; or to distance itself from the problem by disavowing any responsibility or refusing to see that a problem exists at all.

For example, the installation of an AAA-rated shower head in the average Australian household will reduce water usage by at least 20,000 litres and save about half a tonne of carbon dioxide production in a single year. But as the retail plumbing industry already has an established market for shower heads; there is no real incentive for it to push AAA-rated shower heads to a consumer base that is already buying large numbers of inefficient shower heads. And consumers, by and large, want to see the issue of climate change addressed but generally aren't sufficiently motivated to change their individual behaviour, even though it would save them money in the medium term to change, for example, to a more efficient shower head.

Water policy and energy policy are generally the responsibility of two different government departments. These are traditionally fenced off by bureaucratic walls and by a desire to define their role and output distinctively and separately from other departments and tiers of government. Therefore they develop strategies independently of one another. This results in non-action on this issue. Such a situation calls for governments to make a value call: water conservation and carbon emission reductions are a priority, so we will mandate that all homes fit AAA shower heads.

Governments tend to tinker around the edges of many of these issues, reluctant to step up and lead change in these areas. In any debate on policy, battle lines get drawn along old ideological boundaries: social outcomes versus economic outcomes; left versus right; development versus the environment. It is possible, however, to redraw these arguments along very different lines, and it is essential that we do so if we are to achieve a world that is environmentally sustainable and relatively free from poverty.

We need to make a shift to a new paradigm of social and economic policy. We already have the language, but we have only tentatively begun to put into practice the concepts behind it. *Joined-up government, whole-of-government approach, social enterprise, corporate social responsibility, triple bottom line* and *sustainability* are some of the phrases that express this new agenda. Different sectors use different terms, but the language is there and developing rapidly. Some organisations are even putting the ideas encoded in these words into practice. In the last twelve months, awareness of global warming has accelerated this kind of thinking and practice enormously.

Governments have a vital role in creating the conditions under which these practices can flourish. They are, in fact, crucial to establishing a value-centred market economy. Such an economy will exist when all of us adopt a more complex approach to defining value and making that value central to government policy, business practice and the choices we as individuals make about what we buy and how we live. Value-centred market economics can work within the structures and mechanisms that we already have. I'm not advocating the overthrow of capitalism—that battle was lost long ago—merely a broader definition of value that includes the environmental and social impact of the decisions and actions of individuals, businesspeople, non-government organisations, corporations, politicians and policy makers.

Governments set the agenda and define the values to which we as a society aspire. Through policy decisions, legislation and regulation, governments can set the stage for creative and dynamic responses to the values they articulate and champion.

Increasing numbers of companies are adopting this new language and the way of thinking that it represents. In 2007, Westpac, Toyota, Rio Tinto, ANZ and BHP Billiton all appeared in the top ranks of Australia's Corporate Responsibility Index, which assesses the systems businesses use to achieve best practice in the areas of community, environment, marketplace and workplace. In the wake of Sir Nicholas Stern's report on the likely economic impact of global warming, leading businesses are calling for a carbon tax, and many businesses, both small and large, are striving to improve their performance in areas such as community investment, environmental issues, diversity and work–life balance. There is a growing recognition, too, that corporate social responsibility benefits businesses as well as the community.

Welfare organisations are also beginning to explore alternatives to the ways they have traditionally operated. Significant work and research is being done in the areas of social enterprise and corporate partnerships. In Australia, remote Aboriginal communities are forging relationships with corporations in an effort to create employment and business opportunities. The work the Pearson brothers, Noel and Gerhardt, are doing in Cape York, Queensland, with Westpac and the Boston Consulting Group and others is one example of this (see page 67). Many philanthropic agencies are exploring new ways of working with the market and with industry players to effect lasting change in the areas of job creation and poverty reduction. The Brotherhood of St Laurence has created partnerships with bodies such as the ANZ Bank to offer loans to people on low incomes, and with the Victorian Office of Housing to employ residents of public housing to provide services such as security and cleaning in their buildings.

Of course, there are many who say that these partnerships and modes of corporate behaviour are just old ideas rehashed or rebadged. They are wrong. These models are different because they are being developed in a new century with changing technologies, fresh insights, unique problems and different people. Of course we can use lessons from the past, but in the main we need fresh approaches. It is time, confronted by ongoing poverty and environmental degradation as we are, to suspend our cynicism and at least contemplate different ways of operating. Let us use all our combined skills and experience to end these blights on society. Let us create lasting solutions to these seemingly intractable problems of poverty, injustice and environmental damage.

For fifteen years I have been pleased to be called a social entrepreneur. A social entrepreneur is not merely someone who is innovative in terms of delivering a service while still relying for funding on philanthropic donations or government grants. A true social entrepreneur locates the interface between a social goal and building a consumer base for that service that delivers that goal. Some of the experiences that have developed my skills in, and my ideas about, working in this way include growing up as part of a successful family business, my economic qualifications, and my early years in the corporate sector, including some time as a stockbroker.

The term social entrepreneur also reflects my commitment to caring for people and the planet; my work in the not-for-profit sector as the founder of several organisations; my becoming an Anglican priest and leading the Brotherhood of St Laurence, one of Australia's most significant welfare agencies. More recently, being a social entrepreneur led me to establish Easy Being Green and Cool **nrg**, for-profit companies that aim to use the market to promote reduction in carbon emissions within Australia and globally. Now, with Cool **nrg**, I want to create a business model of international significance that embraces the ideal of value-centred market economics.

As a social entrepreneur, I have striven to move beyond the confines of business, charity, poverty and philanthropy to a way of working defined by this new language. What I have come to realise is that we will only overcome our problems by ensuring that all citizens get a chance to participate in change, and using the market is the best way to do this. We have to create the opportunities for change in a global, market-driven economy. We will have to let go of our old, safe, comfortable boundaries and well-rehearsed rhetoric in order to work together. We will need new partnerships, friendships and relationships to help us implement the values and achieve the outcomes we aspire to. We will need to challenge all our long-held beliefs to make these real changes.

I left the Brotherhood of St Laurence at the end of 2003. I had come to the conclusion that charity couldn't deliver the outcomes I was trying to achieve: primarily, the alleviation of poverty. I had done well out of the business of welfare. I had a very good salary and a company car. I was in the comfortable position of being able to feel righteous: Father Nic Frances, MBE, Anglican priest, warrior for the poor and downtrodden. When I approached government and business, I was able to use this righteousness to demand money: 'The welfare sector is good and we are doing what is right. You, on the other hand, are bad, but you can redeem yourself by giving us money.'

And they did give us money. Millions of dollars. It still wasn't enough to solve the problem, but it was enough for business and government to assuage their guilt and enough for us to continue to feel good about ourselves: we were fighting poverty.

That's what I call the cycle of separateness.

The sobering thing, however, was that after five years as the CEO of one of Australia's most successful charities, I realised that the Brotherhood was only meeting a tiny fraction of the needs in the communities in which we operated. When the Brotherhood began in the 1930s, 80 per cent of the community it strove to assist were unemployed. In 2003, when I resigned from the Brotherhood, 80 per cent of people in the Housing Commission flats across the road from our office were still unemployed.

Seventy years on, not only were the problems of those we had pledged to help almost unchanged, but we had not shifted the debate about poverty or alleviated the plight of indigenous Australians. Even more dishearteningly, we had not eliminated many of the factors contributing to poverty or identified any lasting solutions. Some groups, it's true, have been greatly helped by the activity of welfare agencies or by policy changes in particular areas. But the poor remain, and the environment continues to be exploited.

I began to see that we at the Brotherhood, along with the rest of the welfare sector, were culpable. We had become caught up in being virtuous. We were as much to blame as big business and government. We had taken on the responsibility for alleviating poverty and injustice and we had failed. The problem was that we had a seventy-year history of feeling good about ourselves. I myself had been caught up in it. Much of my self-esteem was built on the belief that I was a good person because I was trying to help the poor. We at the Brotherhood had a huge investment in this belief and in not shifting from it.

I realised that we were so passionate about our jobs and our place in the scheme of things, about being on the radio and talking loud and long about poverty, that we were not willing to let go of our ideologies or our position to achieve real justice.

I also saw that all of us—the welfare sector, the environmental movement, business, government and the community as a whole—had become stuck in entrenched positions that prevent meaningful debate about the problems that confront us.

Faced with these realisations, I felt I had no choice but to resign. I decided that I wanted to run a business and use the market to achieve a social end. Two years after establishing Easy Being Green, I had created more jobs than the Brotherhood of St Laurence had done in my five years there as CEO.

Creating employment for the poor and disadvantaged was one of our main goals at the Brotherhood, yet a good business idea executed well could have provided more jobs and cost less money than we spent as a charity. If we had spent the Brotherhood's budget on setting up social enterprises, we could have increased our job placement rate twenty times over. Yet there was a real resistance within the Brotherhood to exploring structural change.

Charity just isn't enough. Charity is, sadly, only ever the leftovers—the spare cash—and leftovers are never going to be enough to solve all the problems of the world. I'm advocating the end of charity, because it is not driving change. Charity and welfare support the status quo. The gap between rich and poor is getting wider, with dire consequences at both ends of the spectrum. We are all more alienated; we are all more frightened. We have to find solutions that make a difference. It is about justice, and justice is bigger than ideology.

In Australia, we are facing some clearly defined issues that need resourcing: long-term entrenched unemployment, the degradation of our public education system, the management of our water resources, quality care for older people, salination and deforestation, drought and global warming, the growing gap between rich and poor, lack of quality childcare, and the alienation of minority groups and communities. The UK, US and Europe are facing similar issues. Across the globe, people are becoming more and more cynical about government's ability or willingness to tackle the problems that confront us.

Yet there is very little debate about the goals most of us would agree are crucial for a just and sustainable world: a clean environment; efficient, renewable energy; a quality education system accessible to all; opportunities for those in need to help themselves. If we can make a market case for these goals and for developing ways to achieve them, we will be on our way to lasting change.

How do we create a market for positive social change? For a start, we have to price the things we want to achieve according to their value and the cost of not having them. They cannot be priced according to ideology or historic preference. For example, subsidising the cost of electricity generated by brown coal, a major polluter, while not subsidising hydro, solar or wind power or energy efficiency to the same extent forces us to remain polluters and undermines the market's ability to self-correct. Providers of goods and services from all sectors need to formulate a more complete value proposition—one that includes the benefits and the costs of their product—whether it is energy, training for the unemployed, or fertiliser.

Governments have a vital role here. In the UK, Gordon Brown, only weeks after he became Prime Minister, announced plans to persuade EU member countries to reduce taxes on environmentally friendly products to make them cheaper and so more attractive to consumers. Sadly, he was ultimately thwarted by a powerful German industry lobby group. In the area of welfare and assistance for the unemployed, tax reform is another area where governments can act. Taking the tax burden off those on low incomes would encourage the transition from welfare to work. If their wages were exempt from income tax, unemployed people would have more incentive to work even a few hours a week, and the revenue lost to government would be minimal.

In this book, I want to suggest ways in which we can link issues and their solutions to build stronger shared values, reduce the number of people excluded from the mainstream and take on some of the pressing issues of our time. This can be done at little or no extra cost to government and business, and could actually increase our gross domestic product. Just as important, these solutions can give us hope as well as the experience and knowledge to help lead the world in tackling these problems.

The various sectors—government, private enterprise, welfare and non-government organisations—are almost ready to do this kind of work. Each has been moving separately to this point. The language is there and the practice has begun, but each sector is still bound by its allegiances to past ways of operating. I have recently been using the phrase *spirited sustainability* to describe ways of working that are clearly looking towards a sustainable future, because to achieve a sustainable future we have to make a leap of faith. We need faith in ourselves and in each other. We will have to become spiritual warriors, standing up for what we value and for each other.

2

The Furniture Resource Centre: Discovering the principles of value-centred market economics

In 1988, having turned my back on stockbroking as a career, I developed an interest in 'Christian socialism'. I had become aware of the work of Neville Black, a priest in Liverpool, UK, who was working with the homeless and other disadvantaged people. I decided to move to Liverpool to assist Neville with his work.

Initially my ambitions were very vague. I knew I wanted to explore my own capacity to live differently and to expose myself to a broader range of views and experiences than those that had previously been open to me as a privileged young man determined to make myself wealthy.

I did a range of voluntary activities in those early days in Liverpool, including running the local youth club for the Anglican Church in Toxteth, illegally putting up posters for the Unemployed Union about protest marches, opening the church at night as a coffee shop for the local prostitutes, and doing the 'God slot' for Neville at the local school on a Wednesday morning. I also visited people in need of assistance in their homes and was shocked to find that many of them lacked the most basic household items.

In my naivety, I had no idea that in the country where I was born and had grown up so many people lived with so little. In our church community, more than half the people were unemployed. Many of these people were living in houses without basic essentials such as stoves, refrigerators, washing machines, tables, chairs, heating or even beds. I was appalled. Without these basic items, finding work, studying or training, even getting children off to school was nearly impossible. Without a bed to sleep in, a table to eat off, a chair to sit on, how could these people hope to lead a normal life?

An idea began to crystallise in my mind: I would set up a large furniture resource centre where homeless and disadvantaged people could get the household items they needed quickly and with efficient and professional service. The journey this enterprise would take me on illuminated the principles of achieving social change that inform my business practices today.

SOLUTIONS ON A LARGE SCALE

At the first meeting to discuss the setting up of the Furniture Resource Centre (FRC), I was proud of my initiative and full of my own importance: I had identified a need in the parish and I was going to provide for that need. It took just one comment from an elderly parishioner to bring me back to earth.

'You're clearly a very nice young man,' she told me kindly, 'and I have no doubt that you will be able to do some very good things for some people in this community. But never forget that for every single person you help there will be ninety-nine out there needing assistance. Before you congratulate yourself for the good you're going to do, think how you're going to use that experience to help the other ninety-nine, because only then will you really have achieved change.'

Those words set the stage for the way I was going to work from then on. I was determined that the FRC would not only meet people's immediate needs but also aim to assist people out of poverty and disadvantage and, crucially, be a model that could be replicated and expanded—not just in Liverpool, but across the UK.

APPLYING BUSINESS PRINCIPLES TO SOCIAL GOALS

The FRC was not a new idea. At least a dozen organisations in Liverpool were collecting secondhand furniture and recycling it or distributing it to people in need. However, these organisations were extremely inefficient.

They were of three main types: charitable and anti-poverty groups; those offering retraining or employment for the long-term unemployed; and environmental groups, whose paramount motivation was recycling.

The recyclers were an interesting group. Their centres were overflowing with furniture in all states of disrepair because nothing was ever refused. Recycling was the goal for them, in and of itself, and they would foist no end of rubbish—shoddy and even hazardous items—on people simply because 'the poor' needed furniture and giving them this stuff was better than throwing it away.

For this group, their passion for the ideal of recycling

seemed to outweigh all other concerns. They were willing to exploit their workers and lose money for themselves and others simply to achieve the outcome of recycling. Other, longer-term goals, such as moving people out of poverty and providing them with employment opportunities—or even promoting environmentalism and recycling as a viable solution to waste issues and exploitation of natural resources—seemed of no importance to them. Certainly the work they were doing was not innovative, nor was it substantially changing the way the individuals they were 'helping' lived or the way the community as a whole operated.

Anti-poverty organisations were trying to redistribute furniture of high quality, but they relied on gifts of money to ensure that they could collect the items and then redistribute them. The biggest of these in Liverpool was the St Vincent de Paul Society. Its aim was simply to help the poor. It supported and ran a large furniture recycling depot, but without much professionalism. The quality of the products was poor, as there simply wasn't enough money available to supply better ones. Its volunteers were, I believe, poorly looked after and the stuff they distributed was, in some cases, worse than rubbish.

In Liverpool, I found that recycling within employment or training schemes worked the best because these bodies were actually creating opportunities for the unemployed. They had managers overseeing the trainees, and health and safety issues tended to be taken seriously. However, as they paid little attention to the cost of recycling or quality of the product, they were able to survive only through government funding.

What made all the existing groups particularly unhelpful, in my opinion, was that many of them had little regard for the people they purported to be helping. It seemed that delivering something to 'the poor', regardless of whether it was useful or valuable, was their prime motivation.

The trouble was that recycling products or selling them secondhand is hard to sustain. By the time an item is collected, repaired and stored—even if all the labour is done by volunteers—the margin between its value or sale price and what it has cost to acquire is minimal. This meant that only the most efficient organisations could survive.

The better organisations, I felt, were those that were selling their products. This forced them to make decisions about what furniture was worth keeping and reselling and which items it was better simply to dump in a hole in the ground. The organisations that were recycling good-quality furniture in an efficient and cost-effective way were the exceptions, but even they had no concept of marketing plans or business models—they were just doing 'good works'.

From the outset, I decided that the FRC would incorporate business practices and that our ability to operate within market realities would determine our success or failure. This, I believed, would also help attract philanthropic and government support.

IDENTIFYING TRUE VALUE/COST IN THE MARGINS

I developed a business plan for the Furniture Resource Centre and put together several applications for founding grants to help us secure premises in Toxteth, an inner-city area, and buy a vehicle to collect secondhand furniture. Eventually, after jumping through a few hoops, we attracted the funding we needed and the project began. The FRC set up outlets for the furniture we collected and began selling it to those who needed it. Such was our success that we took over several other charitable ventures offering a similar service. Soon the demand for furniture outstripped our ability to supply it, and we looked around for alternative sources.

Liverpool City Council also collected unwanted furniture. It had a fleet of ten trucks that would pick up hard rubbish at residents' request. Often the stuff would be taken straight to the tip by the council workers, who would sell anything worthwhile to antique dealers on the way. I proposed that the FRC take over the service. We would salvage useable goods and recycle them; the rest we would deliver to the tip. This scheme would benefit not only the FRC but the council and the whole community. Running the service would provide an opportunity for the FRC to employ and train long-term unemployed people; the council's recycling figures would improve; our costs would be reduced by selling some of the collected items; the service would be better and more efficient; and we would be able to offer a low-cost product to the poor. After much lobbying the council finally agreed to our proposal, and our business started to thrive.

The catalyst for our success was a law passed during that time regarding the disposal of chlorofluorocarbons (CFCs), the cooling gases in refrigerators. Previously the council had been crushing old refrigerators before disposing of them. That practice would now incur a £20,000 fine. Instead, the law required that they collect the CFCs before the refrigerators were compacted.

As part of our deal with the council, we offered to collect the refrigerators that residents were throwing out, de-gas them, reuse the CFCs in those refrigerators worth salvaging, and dispose of the remainder in an environmentally responsible way. The council would avoid potential fines and save on the cost of collection and de-gassing. The FRC would provide a more efficient recycling service, create jobs, meet an environmental imperative, and do it all in a more cost-effective way.

Before the FRC took it over, hard rubbish collection for the Liverpool Council had simply been a cost that it absorbed. The FRC was able to identify the margin of value in that hard rubbish—furniture that was in good enough condition to be resold. In addition, we were able to hire and train previously unemployed people to do the work. Suddenly, by bringing together the problems of waste product disposal, unemployment, the need to train the unemployed, and the need to provide furniture to the disadvantaged, we had made connections and created new value. Where before there had simply been costs—the cost of disposal, of providing furniture, of paying unemployment benefits, of training—there were now value and opportunities—a training opportunity, a job opportunity, a recycling opportunity.

THE VALUE OF INTUITION AND ORGANIC PROCESSES

A major issue for the disadvantaged in Toxteth was the high cost of electrical appliances. We often picked up such goods as part of our collection service, but they generally needed maintenance or repair. The FRC had no one who was skilled in this area, so most of these goods simply went to the tip.

One day I delivered a refrigerator and a stove to a Nigerian man, Parkerson Otti. He wept as the items were installed. He explained that he was a highly qualified electrician who had worked in the Nigerian Navy. Now the only job he was able to get was as a poorly paid night security guard on a building site. This meant he could be at home with his children during the day, but at night he had to leave them in the flat by themselves. He'd set up an intercom connection to his neighbours' flat in case his kids woke up in the middle of the night when he was away. I immediately saw the solution to both our problems: I offered to employ Parkerson to renovate electrical products. With a huge grin, he agreed.

Parkerson brought great professionalism to his job, and soon he was training others. We had the potential for a big project here—not only for Liverpool, but a model that could be replicated elsewhere. There was a great need for these products, and many of them were simply ending up as landfill. If we could get the collection part right, we could make a really big contribution—to training, to employment, to recycling and to helping those in poverty.

Our success at the FRC was partly due to our flexibility: we could respond quickly to change and to opportunities as they presented themselves. Rather than working on some hypothetical scenario or conforming mindlessly to a strategy worked out by a committee in some boardroom, we were responding directly to the situation and the community in which we found ourselves. On meeting Parkerson and being confronted with his need, his passion, his poverty, his skills and his experience, I was able to act on my gut response: here was someone who could add real value to the FRC and for whom a skilled job would make an enormous difference.

BUILDING REAL PARTNERSHIPS

This world of supplying goods and services to the needy that I had entered was badly under-resourced. It was a world where 'doing good' involved little management or training and rarely delivered lasting change. I suddenly realised I had skills that had rarely been put at the service of these communities: skills in marketing, business, management, finance, advertising, PR, communication.

I began to use what I had learned in business with my family and as a stockbroker to build the FRC. To be successful, the FRC would need to forge strong partnerships. For these partnerships to endure the tough times, our partners needed not only to be clear about what they were doing for us, but to understand and appreciate the benefits of working with the FRC. It had to be a two-way street.

To support Parkerson's work repairing and maintaining appliances, I applied for funding to set up an electrical recycling unit. We needed £80,000. We were already spending £80,000 a year on furniture, so this meant doubling the size of the organisation. I sent my proposal to many philanthropic organisations, including the Gold Exchange, an old-fashioned London establishment. The Gold Exchange operates as a guild for gold traders, and the Chancellor of the Exchequer was its treasurer. To my surprise, it sent two representatives to interview me. I showed them around the Furniture Resource Centre; they were impressed. Then they took me out to lunch. We went to the top hotel in Liverpool, which I had never set foot in. You could tell these guys were from London. They took one look at the wine list and asked the waiter, 'What have you got in the cellar that you're not telling us about?' After years away from this world, I could barely concentrate on the fact that I was hoping to persuade these two men to give me £80,000 so I could continue to alleviate poverty. All I could think was, 'Please, give me another glass of that extraordinary claret.'

The meal went well, and at a certain point I knew that the deal was almost done: these guys were going to give me the money. So I asked them, 'What can the FRC do for you in return for the £80,000?'

They both looked a little nonplussed. 'Just take the £80,000,' they said. 'We don't require anything from you.'

It was my turn to look nonplussed. 'You're from London,' I said. 'You'll be investing in a project in Liverpool that is about recycling, about employment, about job creation, about the environment. Those should be important issues for the members of the Gold Exchange. How can we tell your members about them?'

'There's nothing you can tell our members.'

'Hang on a minute,' I replied, 'you've got the Chancellor of the Exchequer as your treasurer. He's part of the government. It's really important to tell our story to some of these decision makers, because it might influence their policy.'

They were losing patience. 'Look, Nic, we're offering you £80,000. Take it. Develop something and we'll write it up. You don't need to teach us anything.'

Suddenly I knew I was going to refuse the grant. 'What a shame,' I was thinking. 'I'm not going to get to enjoy the rest of this meal or have another glass of that wonderful claret, because I'm about to suggest that these people have something to learn.'

Taking money from the very people who were behind the policies that contribute to poverty to help twenty, thirty, or even a thousand people while doing nothing to alleviate the suffering of another 59,000 in the rest of the country was, I decided, just not worth it.

It was a big leap: I realised that it was not enough simply to take charity. Charity allowed people to continue operating in unjust ways. What we were doing to help one person in poverty, as the elderly parishioner had pointed out at that initial meeting, had to help all people living in poverty. If the FRC said yes to this money, we would be letting these powerful people off the hook. I was determined that the FRC would enter only into relationships that allowed us to fully participate as equal partners. Eventually, such relationships would come.

CHARITY IS NOT ENOUGH

During the next three years the FRC tried a range of things to guarantee the funding we needed to continue. We aimed to run our furniture seconds business at a profit. However, while the better-quality items and the knick-knacks sold well, we still had to rely on philanthropic gifts. We were able to attract those gifts because of the quality of our service, the way we treated our staff, the care we took with our products and our focus on our customers and end users.

By the end of those three years it seemed to me that the need for our services was as great as ever, yet we were still meeting only a small part of it. I also felt that it was time to move on. I had resolved when I started the project that it would eventually be run by local unemployed people. I decided to hand it over to my capable deputy, Robbie Davison.

I took a job as a regional fund raiser with Christian Aid, an international aid agency, and it was there that I began to truly grasp the role charity played in maintaining poverty and disadvantage.

My role at Christian Aid revolved around payroll giving: people would offer to donate a certain sum from their weekly wage to a charity. I was excited about exploring this idea: if we were to really cut into poverty, then we all needed to be involved. Working people needed to acknowledge that not only their taxes, but their earnings could make a difference to others. I saw payroll giving as a way of encouraging people's sense of community. I also felt it was important for companies to offer this opportunity to their staff.

But the work left me disillusioned. From the start companies failed to understand the concept of community involvement. They were not interested in making that commitment. Payroll deductions were made by individuals in organisations, but never by the organisations themselves. In terms of advancing an agenda of corporate responsibility, the scheme did nothing. Payroll giving allowed people to say, 'Here's my £10—now I feel OK.' Worse, Christian Aid was satisfied with that.

I was disappointed that Christian Aid failed to challenge people about their politics, the way they lived or how they interacted with their community. We were not calling on people to do anything but part with their cash. We didn't challenge them about how they lived in case they stopped funding us. We let them off the hook.

I realised that charity in this form would never affect the fundamental causes of poverty.

Generally, people did not give to charity out of love but as a way of making themselves feel better. They could hold on to their privilege, their money, their position, their power over others simply by giving away crumbs from their table. After three years at the Furniture Resource Centre, I knew there was no charity in giving rubbish to somebody in need.

If somebody has no bed it might be appropriate to offer them a stained mattress. They may feel they have no choice but to accept it. Will they feel grateful to the giver? Perhaps—or maybe they'll just feel resentful that once again their dignity has been overlooked. The only person likely to feel good about this transaction is the one who gave away an old, stained mattress that he might just as well have taken to the tip. Certainly, the person he gave it to now feels as if she's truly at the bottom of the heap. Using such a transaction to feel better about oneself seems abusive rather than charitable to me.

THE MARKET AS A MECHANISM FOR SOCIAL CHANGE

Two years after I joined Christian Aid, the FRC, under the management of Robbie Davison, was delivering twice as much furniture for the same amount of money. It did its job well and was getting better at doing it, but the world was changing and the FRC needed to change with it. I had stayed good friends with Robbie, and he asked me to come back as chair of the FRC board. I agreed to return for a year to really scrutinise the service the FRC provided and to promote its development. Robbie continued in his management role and I had an opportunity, with him, to start confronting the issues of poverty and charity from a wholly new perspective.

My time at Christian Aid had cemented my belief that the only meaningful way to assist the disadvantaged was via the market. We had to weigh the costs to our society of people being denied the resources they needed to take their place as fully contributing citizens. These costs were huge:

unemployment, theft, vandalism, drug use, suicide, gambling, homelessness, fear and desperation. Yet the community had never measured them. Our calculations took into account how much it cost us to *help* the homeless but not what it cost to *keep* them homeless. I was determined that we at the FRC would begin to measure poverty financially. To do this we would have to become a different type of organisation. The key to that would be our ability to forge partnerships outside the welfare sector.

The Furniture Resource Centre had to be about new furniture. Despite some opposition from within the organisation, I approached Barry McKenzie, the financial controller of Silent Nights, the biggest UK manufacturer of beds, and asked him to become the FRC's main bed supplier. 'No problem,' he said. 'I'll give you a hundred new beds for next year.'

'That's great,' I said. 'But, Barry, we want 5000 beds.'

Barry did a double take, 'Nic, we don't *sell* 5000 beds to any one single customer. We can't possibly *give* that many away.'

'You don't understand, Barry,' I told him. 'I don't want you to give me anything—I want you to sell me 5000 beds. And I want you to give the FRC the best rate in the country for a single bed, as if we were already your biggest and best customer.'

Now I was talking his language—I was talking business. Barry had been willing to give the FRC 100 beds for free, but negotiating a deal—giving us the biggest discount, letting commercially sensitive information outside his office—was a very different ball game.

Initially Barry was sceptical that we could achieve our aim of selling thousands of beds in a year. The community we intended to sell to—the poor and unemployed—hardly seemed a significant or reliable consumer base. Over two or three meetings, however, we were able to convince Barry that we could build a market in this community and that the FRC could become a major customer. Silent Nights would also benefit from working with a charity by demonstrating that it was a good corporate citizen.

Barry came through with high-quality single and double beds at the lowest price in the country. Within five years the FRC delivered on our promise: we had become one of Silent Nights' biggest customers.

Our next project was to set up a similar partnership with a supplier of electrical goods. I had received a tip-off that Jim Donovan, head of corporate affairs and human resources at Thorn EMI, one of the UK's 100 top companies, was checking out Liverpool. Thorn was looking for ways to recycle its ex-rental stock: items such as washing machines, stoves and televisions. The government, in the light of environmental concerns about the disposal of such products, was pressuring the company to find an alternative to simply using them as landfill. Thorn was looking to improve its environmental credentials by making these goods available to the disadvantaged.

I tracked down the man who was organising Jim Donovan's itinerary and managed to convince him to arrange a visit to the FRC. I was determined that by the end of Donovan's visit our electrical business would be working hand-in-hand with Thorn EMI.

All that we had learned over the years was about to be applied in proposing a partnership with this corporate giant. The FRC had been scrabbling around with a couple of old trucks asking people to give us their old cookers. As Donovan walked through the door, I saw a chance to secure not just all the white goods we needed, but also the skills to repair and rebuild these products on a large scale.

Parkerson had been rebuilding cookers with precision and loving care, but we needed to take the operation to a new level. To do that we needed Thorn's resources, but we also had things to offer Donovan. The FRC had experience in recycling products and knowledge of the low-income consumer base—the kind of people who needed these products, how they needed them and why. We also had experience in recruiting long-term unemployed people and providing them with skills and meaningful work. Our expertise in this area, combined with Thorn's in the industrial area, would make us even more successful in placing previously unemployed people into real jobs. Donovan and I both realised we were two sides of what could become a unique and interesting business partnership.

We explored lots of different options and ended up setting up a project in Speke which, along with Toxteth, is one of the most deprived areas in the UK. Our venture, CREATE, would sell reconditioned ex-rental goods to low-income households and provide training and jobs to long-term unemployed people. It received support from the European Regional Development Fund, the national government, local government, and other manufacturers and sponsors that Thorn brought on board.

Thorn put £250,000 on the table, and the FRC put in £500,000 obtained through its links to government networks and contacts that Thorn couldn't have accessed without us. The FRC was as big a player in the deal as Thorn was, not just financially but in terms of our knowledge of the product and the customer.

Culturally, the FRC and Thorn EMI were poles apart, but in this project we were finding common ground. By the time CREATE was solidly established, I counted Jim as a good friend.

The project became part of Thorn's core business—to the extent that CREATE featured prominently in the company's annual report. Thorn could now say to its shareholders, its customers and the community at large: 'If you want to know what kind of organisation Thorn EMI is, how well we listen to people, what values we aspire to, look at our CREATE project.'

The involvement in CREATE also influenced Thorn's corporate culture. Jim told me that CREATE fundamentally changed the way Thorn viewed its 1100 staff. Training unemployed people, employing them and seeing their commitment to their work forced the company to rethink the way it treated its regular employees and changed the way it viewed its customers and their needs.

This partnership was profound in more ways than I could have envisioned. The level of professionalism and skills we brought to the welfare sector changed it forever. And not just in one isolated community—the changes were happening all over Britain.

Just as significantly, in my view, Jim said he hadn't had as much fun since his university days. I had the sense that this passionate man was also proud of the work he was doing with us. Through CREATE, both Thorn EMI and the FRC had moved beyond mere 'business' or 'welfare'. We were working together, changing society for the better. Finally, the partnerships I had envisioned all those years ago were a reality.

John had worked for years as a volunteer at one of the St Vincent de Paul furniture stores the Furniture Resource Centre took over. He had a bunch of kids, some of whom —like him—had spent time in prison. Now in his mid-fifties, John was illiterate and had only ever had sporadic work as a labourer. If one of his kids got sick or needed a pair of shoes, John might nick a thing or two to make ends meet. But his heart was in the right place, so he worked for nothing at St Vincent de Paul giving away broken-down furniture to people in much the same boat as himself.

When the FRC took over, John offered to stay on as a volunteer in the new set-up. We didn't use volunteers. Instead we offered John a job. Initially, he did much the same work as he had done for St Vincent de Paul. However, we also offered him training. Among other things, he learned to drive and got his licence. It became obvious that John had a knack for communicating with and mentoring the younger men who worked at the FRC: his own sons had given him lots of experience in dealing with teenage boys. We asked him to become a trainer.

John took on the task with enthusiasm. He realised that the young men learning to work on the trucks collecting furniture didn't know how to be safe; they took unnecessary risks as a matter of course. John asked me if he could become a health and safety officer for the FRC. I was impressed by his initiative but pointed out that his illiteracy would make it impossible for him to fulfil the requirements of such a role.

His answer stunned me. 'I've learned how to read and write,' he said. 'I can do it.'

On his own initiative, at the age of fifty-five, with no record of secure employment before his association with the FRC, John had taken it upon himself to learn to read and write so he could become a health and safety officer. In the space of a few years, on the back of a job that was real and meaningful, John had not only lifted himself out of poverty, he had completely re-invented himself and was mentoring others on how to make that journey.

COMPLEX MARKETS

Traditionally, markets have been understood in simple, binary terms: buyers and sellers; supply and demand; producers and consumers. It didn't take long for me to realise, however, that the market model in which the FRC operated was in fact multi-dimensional.

Our aim was simple: provide disadvantaged people with furniture and other household goods. Initially, we did this in a very straightforward way: the goods went from us as the supplier to the poor as the consumers. Within a few years, however, the relationships and number of players in this exchange had changed dramatically.

Rather than giving furniture directly to those who needed it, we often sold it to landlords to put in low-cost accommodation. That allowed landlords to ask for higher rents—but the government also increased homeless people's social security payments when they moved into furnished accommodation. Our research showed that previously homeless tenants stayed longer in furnished than in unfurnished accommodation. The government agencies recognised that keeping previously transient tenants in accommodation for longer reduced their costs, which included vandalism, lost rent and the expense of finding new tenants. The costs of supporting the homeless were also reduced. Because our operation was efficient and cost effective we were able to offer training and jobs to the unemployed. This also reduced the cost to local government of providing and funding training schemes. By taking over hard-rubbish collection, we also saved councils the cost of providing this service.

There were more intangible benefits which are difficult to assess because the changes are so profound: a more stable community, for example, and more environmentally sustainable practices. The FRC was also using suppliers who themselves were creating social value by employing and training the disabled or mentally ill. The transactions and relationships formed an ever stronger web that supported many people and created value in many areas and whose size and impact expanded exponentially.

LESSONS LEARNED

The Furniture Resource Centre had started in Toxteth, but from the beginning we aimed to serve a much wider area. First we expanded our operation throughout Liverpool, then extended all over northwest England. By the time I left, we were supplying furniture from London to Glasgow.

We were no longer a community business. We had developed a *social business* that met social needs for jobs and local empowerment. We had developed solutions and models that could be employed across the country. We had more than achieved our aim of helping people who were desperate to create a home obtain high-quality furniture that was built and delivered by people who had long been unemployed.

Since I left the organisation in 1997, the FRC has continued to grow and develop. An internationally recognised model of social business with an annual turnover in the millions of pounds, it now comprises a furnishing and removal business, a retail business and a waste management and recycling service. It also offers advice and guidance for others wanting to set up similar enterprises.

The FRC often copped criticism from others in the welfare sector: 'Look at you, you bastards: you pay your staff; you've got company cars, and we can't even phone up for a secondhand—and probably stained—mattress for the homeless any more.'

My reply was, 'No, but you can get them a brand-new bed.'

It wasn't charity any more, and it didn't look like the welfare of the past: more people were getting jobs through the FRC, many of them were getting off the dole for the first time in years, and more people were getting served in a far better way.

Looking back, I now see the experience of setting up the FRC and being part of its evolution as a watershed. It was critical in developing my ideas on social entrepreneurship and confirmed my belief in what I now term value-centred market economics. The experience formed the bedrock of my conviction that the market can be a means to achieve lasting, far-reaching and (relatively) speedy change.

3

Value-centred market economics: What is it and how is it different?

During my time as CEO of the Brotherhood of St Laurence I tried, unsuccessfully as it turned out, to promote use of my term value-centred market economics. I wanted to begin a wider discussion about the role of the market not just in delivering change but also in achieving the goals, aspirations, needs, desires—the values—that our society sees as crucial to a healthy, sustainable and just community. These values include accessible, quality education and health-care systems; work for all; clean water and air; affordable, sustainable energy; open, democratic government; cultural and religious tolerance; and harmonious, vibrant communities. I hoped, naively perhaps, that giving this concept a name within the chosen framework of the market would help us begin to move towards an economic system that recognised a broader range of values than it had traditionally embraced.

When I suggested the term value-centred market economics to my colleagues at the Brotherhood, however, I encountered strong resistance to the concept as well as to the term itself. The organisation, and the people within it, had developed a culture where the market was the enemy, not an entity to be embraced or engaged with.

There was also a general feeling that the word value reflected only monetary worth: dollars and cents, rather than the more profound ideals at the core of society. I wanted to reclaim it so that value-centred market economics would come to describe the art of doing business sustainably, whether that business was the business of government, commerce or welfare.

I believe that the majority of values can and should be given a price. This is not to demean them, but to enable them to stand their ground and be counted by the market. Putting a price on cultural and religious tolerance, say, is more complicated than pricing milk, but if you turn the notion around it becomes easier: what are the costs of cultural and religious *in*tolerance? These might include civil unrest, vandalism, the need for more policing and, in the extreme case, terrorism.

Market principles are fine for the delivery of goods and services, but government can play a crucial role in pricing goods and services in a way that is consistent with moral and social values, not just financial ones. Those values are what we want when we're at our best. The problem is that we aren't always at our best. I strongly believe that government should put a price on activities that support the common good and a healthy planet, then allow the market to organise around these values and deliver its own efficiencies. This is what I mean by value-centred market economics. I will talk more about the role of government in defining and promoting value in subsequent chapters.

One has to decide what is non-negotiable. For us at SEWA (Self-Employed Women's Association), putting the poor and poorest, especially women workers, at the centre of all our thoughts, efforts and initiatives is non-negotiable. We have faith in organising people, especially women, towards the goal of self-reliance. And we do this through building up membership-based organisations of the poor—led, owned and managed by them.

There are other non-negotiables, too, like truth, integrity, non-violence, respecting all faiths and communities equally, simplicity, etc. We draw our inspiration from Mahatma Gandhi's teachings and how he lived his life. So these are the values we hold dear and adhere to.

We then see how far we can work with other partners in ways to benefit the poor and in ways which will lead us to our goal. Of course, our values and core principles guide us in this and help us decide how and with whom to work.

Mirai Chatterjee, Coordinator of Social Security, Self-Employed Women's Association, India

SEWA is a trade union of poor women who earn a living through their own labour or small businesses. It aims to support its members in achieving full employment and self-reliance.

WHY USE THE MARKET TO ACHIEVE SOCIAL CHANGE?

It may appear from some of the ideas I propose in this book that I am an unabashed admirer of the market and its capacity to deliver what we need and want. In reality, I am extremely ambivalent towards it. On one hand I agree with an old friend who died a couple of years ago. He was a passionate critic of the market because he felt that it broke down communities. Rather than relying on family, neighbours or friends to support us, we can buy that support and everything else we might need. Reduced to being mere consumers, we buy separation from our community and—with a video-game console for each child—separation within the family.

In many ways I agree with his assessment. I can see that the market, the economy and money are at the root of many of our problems. However, I'm also a pragmatist. As a social entrepreneur I believe that the market is the only mechanism that can speedily alleviate the problems our current economic system has created. With the best will in the world, we cannot substantially change the world without engaging the market.

Business has proved that it can respond very quickly to market opportunities. Once you begin to cost values, from clean energy to universal health care, business will find a way to develop markets and produce products to feed the demand for those values. Given that socialism failed and capitalism triumphed, the market is the most effective tool we have to address the huge problems inherent in our very flawed system.

That's what I love about the market: that it can be manipulated—if you're clever about it—and used to promote social values. It is crucial that we stop seeing the market as a global beast that we can't control and start seeing it as a tool.

The market is amoral: it honours profit, it honours money; it does not honour social values. Individuals, communities, corporations and governments, however, can and do operate within a moral framework. It is not just possible but imperative for the market to reflect this if we are to effectively tackle social inequity, climate change and poverty. Because of a lack of leadership—and I'll talk more about leadership later—money and greed predominantly drive decision making throughout the world. Until we face that and broaden our goals and our definition of value, very little will change.

That said, how might we change the market so that it reflects more complex values without upsetting the very structure of society and the economy? How do we achieve this shift? Value-centred market economics—incorporating a more complex method of assigning value—can, I believe, facilitate this shift without sending the GDP into a tailspin.

Why the market currently only recognises financial value

We routinely oversimplify complex concepts in order to make sense of them. This is certainly true of the way we define and talk about the economy, and the tendency to simplify this very complex entity risks creating more problems. So, while acknowledging the pitfalls of simplification, I will attempt to briefly outline why greed and the accumulation of wealth have emerged as such powerful drivers of the global economy.

It has become axiomatic that government's primary role and responsibility is to stimulate economic growth. Economic growth creates wealth and improves living standards, and voters will support leaders who deliver these things. Economic prosperity is delivered by companies that use investors' money to grow. The biggest investors are superannuation funds. The managers of these funds keep their jobs by investing in companies that deliver the biggest returns in the shortest time. Unless CEOs deliver short-term growth and profits for their investors, their companies will miss out on investment and they will find themselves out of a job. The average term of a CEO in a single business is three years, and the pressure on them to perform is intense.

Corporate and government decision making is driven overwhelmingly by the same imperative: to ensure that investors or voters—you and I—get a good return for their money or their electoral support. Low interest rates, increased salaries, appreciation of our assets and the homes we've purchased, and growth in our superannuation funds are what most of the decisions of our political and business leaders are aimed at.

The impact of these decisions extends far beyond share prices and interest rates. Those of us who live in the developed world—Europe, the US, Australia, Japan, Canada—demand spiralling economic growth, rarely asking ourselves or our leaders at what cost it comes. But it does come at a cost: to the planet, to the poor, to Third World countries. Resources are exploited, carbon dioxide levels in the atmosphere increase, and fresh water is harder to come by. Yet as long as we, personally, enjoy a rising standard of living we act as if impending disasters and existing injustices are not our responsibility.

Perversely, we then blame our politicians—the very ones we voted for because they promised us personal economic gain. 'Not my fault,' we say. 'I can't change it.' This mindset is so strong that it keeps our politicians running like rats on a treadmill. They don't dare offer visions and values, just economic growth.

In 2005 we consumed Earth's resources at a rate more than double a sustainable level. Ocean fish are being harvested at a level beyond which they can regenerate; carbon dioxide is being pumped into the air at a rate that puts the planet at risk. The growing demand for energy, particularly in the US and Europe, and increasingly China and India, is having an effect on the entire ecosystem. It's not really a concern for the Earth, because Venus and Mars do quite well with very different atmospheres. It is humanity and all the other species we share the planet with for which it is a problem.

Of course, many of us are deeply concerned about the plight of the planet and the poor. Depleted fisheries and shrinking wildlife habitats, the exploitation of the Third World, the disadvantaged and unemployed in our own society who have been sacrificed for productivity gains—all are routinely discussed in the media. But what can we as individuals do? Our politicians present us with a stark choice: 'Vote for us and we'll manage the economy so that we all get richer. Vote for the other lot—who promise environmental sustainability and increased welfare—and they'll blow the budget and you'll find yourself out of a job and with increased interest rates.'

Faced with such bleak alternatives, many of us simply retreat, quietly accepting the reduced view of the world we are presented with. 'I can't risk the well-being of my kids.' 'I can't do anything about the decisions my superannuation fund makes because I'm just one of a million people.' And within those little stories, we continue to support the exploitation of the planet and the people on it at a level that is now clearly unsustainable.

Money itself is not the problem. Money is merely a counter, a token. The problem is how we use money to value some things and not others. We need a way of attributing value that is more complex than looking at the profit sheet of a company or the GDP of a country. We really do need to start valuing in monetary terms those other things that are important to us, like the existence of a planet for our grandchildren.

How do we articulate the new concept of value we want to advocate? What might it look like if we did price social values and put them at the centre of our decision making? It was the FRC that gave me my first experience in doing this. I've taken it much further in my current business venture, Cool nrg.

THE IMPORTANCE OF LEADERSHIP

Mostly, when we think of leadership, we look elsewhere and not within ourselves—to politicians, corporate chiefs and bureaucrats, and, God help us, to celebrities. However, in the years I have been attending the World Economic Forum (WEF) at Davos, Switzerland, along with many international leaders, I have learned that they feel as impotent as you and I—and share the same concerns. They worry about their kids and their lifestyles, and they feel pressured by an electorate or shareholders baying for their blood every few years. Like the rest of us, they are full of good intentions, but they fear they will lose their job if they deviate from the simple economic goal of delivering wealth on a large scale. It doesn't matter who you are—a factory worker or the CEO of a huge conglomerate—the prospect of being sacked, with all the accompanying feelings of failure and humiliation, is always frightening.

Ultimately, we all share the responsibility of living sustainably, of sharing the planet's resources equitably, of ensuring that our children are well educated and instilled with the values of compassion and love. We all have the right, regardless of where we are born or where we live, to wealth, opportunity and housing. It's important that our personal decisions reflect those beliefs and values—that we take them into account when we vote, when we invest our money, and when we have the opportunity to contribute to the debate on these issues. This is what I mean when I talk about spirited sustainability: taking a moral and ethical position and acting in accordance with that position.

Leaders have an even greater responsibility to do this. We must trust other people and be willing to risk our positions and our wealth to enable others to join us. It is not enough to spend twenty or thirty years contributing to the world's problems, then take early retirement and practise philanthropy in order to clean up some of the mess you helped to create. It is the value part of value-centred market economics that leaders can change and policy makers can influence.

At the WEF meeting in Davos in January 2007, I was invited to participate in a dinner session on climate change. I found myself in a room with some of the world's leading thinkers on this issue. During the dinner, some of us were invited to speak for four or five minutes on how we thought WEF delegates could approach the issue.

Among the speakers was Martin Wolf, a former senior economist at the World Bank who now writes for the *Financial Times* in the UK. He spoke eloquently of his conviction, strengthened by his conversations that evening, that the world was facing a massive loss of biodiversity as a result of climate change and that he did not believe we would be able to respond to it in time to avert catastrophe.

His speech was lucid and frightening. But for me the most extraordinary part was when he said he would continue to support current gradual changes in attitudes and actions on climate change even though he didn't think they would make much difference.

I found this most disturbing. That he could believe the situation was dire and was prepared to accept that a catastrophe was inevitable, rather than resolving to use his influence to the utmost to prevent it, left me quite bereft of hope. But that was the tone of much of what I'd heard at the WEF. Again and again there would be agreement: yes, climate change is a huge issue. Yes, it's linked to increased carbon emissions caused by human activity. Yes, it is very urgent. But there's probably nothing significant we can do until 2015, 2020, 2050 because clean coal or nuclear power or large-scale renewable energy will take that long to implement. So although we understood the danger we weren't going to act.

Immediately after Wolf's talk, a US government adviser on climate change launched into a very technical account of the possible response of the White House to this issue. No one challenged Wolf's speech. While a few people discussed the White House's response, the other diners listened in silence. If they were anything like me, they were still reeling from Wolf's admission.

I suddenly realised that my own claim to a leadership role was being challenged at this moment. Here I was, in a room with people I viewed as my peers as leaders of the global response to climate change, and yet words and procrastination, rather than action and energy, were dominating our response. I had two choices: to leave the room and abandon the discussion or to express my rage at the impotence I believed we were choosing.

I grabbed a passing microphone and, interrupting the discussion on the White House's response, asked Wolf, 'Do you mind if I play a kind of game with you now?' He graciously agreed, and I proceeded to rail at the poor man. 'You're in a position of power and influence,' I told him. 'If you know the situation is dire and that our grandchildren's future and much of the planet's biodiversity depend on the actions of the people in this room, not to act immediately in all the ways open to you would in my view leave you open to being charged with crimes against humanity. If we prefer to live comfortably with the status quo rather than to act, we are all responsible for the fate of the planet. We might believe we are the good people because we've been working in this area for some time, but if we are not using all our resources, including our power and status, to take action then I believe we are personally culpable.'

As I sat down, I thought I'd probably blown any chance of ever being taken seriously again by the power brokers and opinion makers in the room. But I really felt that my outburst was the only honourable thing to do. I was heartened by the smattering of applause that followed and even more so when, at the end of the dinner, many of the participants came up to thank me for what I had said.

In leadership terms, the point of social enterprise is to *do* things differently—to act, not simply talk. Faced with urgent issues like climate change or homelessness or AIDS, using all the tools at hand—and particularly markets—to take that action is crucial and imperative.

WHY DOES VALUE-CENTRED MARKET ECONOMICS MEAN THE END OF CHARITY?

The answer has a lot to do with the cycle of separateness that I mentioned earlier. Historically the business of 'good works' has been carried on by welfare agencies and non-government organisations that rely on their members to fund their campaigns. The environmental movement has run very successful campaigns—if you measure success by media attention. But in terms of real change, they've had remarkably little effect. The same can be said for indigenous issues, particularly in Australia; there is a lot of campaigning, commitment, government spending, yet indigenous disadvantage is getting worse. Why might value-centred market economics be different? Is there a way in which the goals of these organisations—furthering the interests of the disadvantaged; preserving wildlife habitat; protecting resources from rampant exploitation—can be given a financial value that allows for economic, market-based solutions as well as environmental and social ones?

We operate in a capitalist framework. If we want to solve a particular problem, we have to be aware of how change comes about in that capitalist framework. This is true whether our goal is eradicating AIDS or promoting classical music. If you understand the economics of the goal you want to achieve—its place within the complex web of cost and benefit—then you can make the case for it and achieve it by engaging the economy and the market.

Governments, too, are focused on GDP, on growth and productivity. In order to get any government onside with a particular objective, a case has to be made for the value this will create—not only social or environmental but economic. This is what we were able to do when we set up the Furniture Resource Centre—make a convincing case to the then Thatcher government that we would not only be employing and training the homeless but saving the government £2000 per homeless person helped per year.

If you run a public company you are answerable to your

investors—mainly financial institutions, as I outlined earlier. Those managing these funds say they are managing them in our interests, but they are only doing so in one of our interests—our financial interest; amassing money for our retirement. The overwhelming majority of business investment is driven by one thing—financial return. As a result, it is very difficult to convince the board of a public company to embrace a strategy that appears to have a social or environmental bias, even if doing so will have a good economic outcome. Partly that's because the outcome is indirect. Board members may have only a couple of hours a month to deal with company issues. A simple profit-driven decision is much easier to make than one involving social and environmental factors, which is inevitably much more complicated.

In Australia over the past twenty years or so, charities have grown very large. One of the biggest charities, the Salvation Army, is also one of the biggest businesses, and it's the same story with similar organisations the world over. But charities seldom have to operate within the real financial world. Rather than tainting themselves with the slightly grubby notions of profit and paying their way, they beg from the corporate world, never having to make a financial case for their existence. They rely on their morally superior position of being concerned with the welfare of the poor, the sick or the environment to avoid having to survive in the marketplace.

Welfare organisations' separation from the marketplace and from commerce renders them impotent because their solutions are developed in a cocoon of money that they've begged from the very companies they demonise as being part of the problem. Structurally, they share a problem with business in that they are generally run by a board of directors who can devote only a couple of hours a month to grappling with the organisation's problems.

I think that the market has its place, but is not the end-all and be-all, as some would have us believe. We cannot leave everything to markets because it is not a level playing field out there. History and experience have taught us that the already better-off countries and people are always the net gainers, often at the expense of the poor. Markets can help, but markets alone are not the only solution, and can even hurt the poor. Thus markets have to be managed to ensure that the poor get a look-in. They have to be managed through policy interventions by governments and multi-lateral organisations.

But there are positive sides to a market economy which even the poor recognise and can use to their benefit. One example is our setting up of insurance services at the Self-Employed Women's Association (SEWA). To ensure that the poor would get the best deal, we invited competitive bids from both government and private insurance companies. SEWA also sells our members' products directly to the market (cutting out the middlemen), thus helping them to increase their income.

In sum, things are not black and white. Markets are not all bad for the poor, nor do they necessarily have bad social outcomes. There are several forces at work. We have to recognise and deal with this. We believe that the only way the poor can ensure a level playing field is to organise—to come together and unite to build their collective strength and bargaining power.

At SEWA, we believe in collective social entrepreneurship led, owned and managed by the poor—preferably women. Social entrepreneurship by itself, led by one or two gifted individuals, is unlikely to bring the kind of social changes we believe in.

Mirai Chatterjee, Coordinator of Social Security, Self-Employed Women's Association, India

Fiduciary responsibility

One of the first things I learned on being appointed CEO of the Brotherhood of St Laurence was that I had a 'fiduciary responsibility' as a board member. This meant that my first responsibility was not to safeguard the interests of the poor but to safeguard the financial assets of the charity. Of course, board members of commercial enterprises also have a fiduciary responsibility. The difference is that a for-profit company has the mechanisms and structures for and, most importantly, the goal of, increasing its financial assets and is prepared to take reasonable financial risks to achieve that goal. A charity, relying as it does on the generosity of others, not only puts its finances at risk when it embarks on a new venture, it also risks losing the ongoing support of donors. Although these risks may be necessary to achieve the broader outcome the organisation wants, board members are loath to take them—after all, their goal is to safeguard the assets of the charity.

I often believed I should be risking everything at the Brotherhood of St Laurence, including the life of the organisation itself, for the rights of the disadvantaged people we were supposed to be fighting for. Yet my board would point out that my responsibility as a director precluded us risking our financial assets, even if taking the safe course compromised our ability to do the work that was our raison d'être.

This posed a dilemma for me. If speaking out publicly against business, for example, jeopardised the future of the organisation, then if I did so I might not be acting responsibly as a director. So fiduciary responsibility limited my ability to do my job. It also meant that we were unable to work on a very large scale but were limited to a more piecemeal approach.

The fiduciary responsibility of the directors of a company also includes overseeing the monitoring of its financial position. For example, every business has to ensure that it remains solvent. However, if accounting systems become overly complex, they can limit the ability of the directors to make good financial decisions. This, I believe, is what happens in large charitable organisations. If too many people are responsible for finances, then tackling issues on a large scale in a fundamental and lasting way and with maximum effect becomes far more difficult, and the charity becomes far less entrepreneurial because of the need for control and probity.

Large welfare organisations often have businesspeople on the board specifically to help them achieve their financial goals. Yet such board members may have taken on the role because they want to 'give back to society', to do 'good work'. The financial risk-taking they normally take in business they do not associate with doing charity. They want to be generous, munificent, not ruthless business operators. They want to act from the heart for a change and, as a result, they often make very poor decisions.

When challenged to think differently, of course they can't. For them it's either black or white: 'my goal is to make a profit' or 'my goal is to do good works'. And even if they do begin thinking about business in a hard-headed way, they only take risks that make sense to them in terms of their financial world. They don't take risks that are complex, involving the consideration of data, goals and values beyond the financial.

When I was at the Brotherhood of St Laurence, we recognised that one of the huge issues for people living in poverty is the difficulty of getting low-cost credit. We approached the ANZ Bank with a scheme to provide people on low incomes with low-interest loans to buy essential household items. (The scheme was launched in a limited form in May 2006, after I left the Brotherhood.)

To deliver low-cost credit to the majority of Australians living in poverty would mean taking on 20 per cent of the entire credit market, which represents about the same market share as one of the four big Australian banks. A well-run micro-credit scheme had the potential not only to provide much-needed assistance to low-income families, but to be a highly profitable business enterprise in its own right.

Despite enthusiasm and support for the scheme on both sides, there were two sizeable obstacles. The first was our cumbersome budgetary process—drawing up a proposal, costing all the elements, developing a time line. This made it difficult to be entrepreneurial in testing the project. While some checks are appropriate, the cost of piloting the project was insignificant considering the overall budget of the Brotherhood. In terms of the project as a whole these processes were necessary, but in terms of innovation they were a hindrance and slowed down our ability to test the project.

Second, even when we'd had some success with the program and saw the potential to roll it out to low-income people around the country, our fear of the sheer scale of this tied us to a small, timid model. It remained linked to one bank and limited to the budget of a 'charitable' rather than a commercial enterprise. Because we feared risking large sums, we created a charitable structure that severely limited the scale of the project. Because of this, while the project is still operating and has won various awards, businesses like Cash Converters and less reputable pawn shops remain the primary bankers to the poor. What's more, the opportunity to establish an ethical, profitable bank whose main customers are the unemployed and the disadvantaged has been forgone.

Because of their fiduciary responsibility to the Brotherhood, the directors effectively said, 'If we turn this scheme into a commercially viable enterprise by offering credit to the financially disadvantaged all around Australia, the amount of debt that we would carry as an organisation would far outweigh our assets and could jeopardise the future of the organisation.' Now, it's appropriate to take that level of risk if you're a bank. For a charity, by contrast, it's not appropriate, so our ability to act like a business was curtailed. Of course a board must take its responsibility for the financial viability of the organisation extremely seriously, but when that responsibility begins to rule the agenda, the ability to act can be crippled.

To find a welfare organisation and its board who are willing to take that kind of risk is almost impossible and may be illegal. Nevertheless, these kinds of schemes, where social entrepreneurship tackles enormous problems, are what is required if social disadvantage is to be addressed in any meaningful way. Mohammad Yunus, of the Grameen Bank in Bangladesh, has been able to achieve this, but in order to shape the business the way he wanted he found he could not have a banker on his board: bankers simply could not grasp the complexity of the mix of outcomes he was trying to deliver.

As I struggle now with the structure of my relatively new business, Cool **nrg**, I have been impressed by those companies that manage to stay entrepreneurial despite their size, particularly the Packer and Murdoch media corporations. On one hand I want a relatively flat, non-hierarchical structure for Cool **nrg** so that my employees feel empowered and involved in the day-to-day operations of the business. On the other hand, I want to maintain control of the business so that I can make quick decisions without jumping too many hurdles of consultation and process. It seems to me that the Packer and Murdoch families have managed for better or for worse to keep a level of control that allows them to move rapidly within their industry in a way unmatched by rival organisations with more complex decision-making processes.

You can find yourself trapped philosophically in business or in welfare. Organisations that are driven by profit have that imperative built into their very structure and are bound by it. Welfare bodies and NGOs that have been set up to do good works are bound by the need to protect the financial base that enables them to continue their work. Their options and outcomes are limited not only by these structural constraints but also by their philosophy and ideology, which prevent them from creating partnerships with business.

Whether the issue you're trying to address is climate change or poverty in Africa, systematic change is needed. Simply throwing money at the problem to fund lobbying or band-aid solutions will ultimately fail. Ending poverty in Africa will take much more structural change than rich countries giving 1 per cent of their wealth. Similarly, lobbying governments is not going to stop climate change: reducing the burning of fossil fuels will. Any response that doesn't achieve that is simply hot air.

Charity's shrinking arena
The arenas where charity can operate effectively are shrinking, and this will continue as social business begins to take up more challenges and more opportunities. The arena of climate change—in which Cool **nrg** operates—is one strikingly obvious example. For a consumer concerned with this

issue, there are several options. You can for example subscribe to an organisation like Greenpeace that lobbies government on this and other issues relating to the environment. Or for around the same cost you can pay a carbon offset provider to offset the carbon emissions you generate. For the same money as you would give to Greenpeace to keep telling people how much of a problem they are, you can become carbon neutral and so stop being part of the problem.

That's what Greenpeace knows how to do—to lobby and campaign—and yet, increasingly, the argument has been won. The business community—especially the larger companies—have acknowledged that climate change is a huge issue and are taking on the challenge of reducing their carbon emissions and insisting governments develop strategies to deal with it. Greenpeace and similar organisations have been successful in helping to shift the agenda somewhat, but they are unable to take it into the mainstream; they remain on the edge of the debate. The solution is action, and the most effective action is in the marketplace. What is the role of an organisation like Greenpeace when their traditional adversaries in business are now taking up their arguments?

Value-centred market economics means the end of charity because charity does not and cannot fundamentally change people's behaviour or the underlying structures that support the status quo. It exists in a bubble of 'doing good', and while that continues it cannot achieve fundamental change. We need a middle-ground solution, and that is where social business comes in.

THE ROLE OF SOCIAL BUSINESS

How do social businesses differ from charities? Traditionally, charities are run on a not-for-profit basis and under a set of rules and regulations that allow them to claim tax benefits and operate under less stringent requirements than business with regard to the employment of staff and other issues. Their income, rather than being self-generated, is generally and predominantly drawn from grants and donations.

Social businesses or social enterprises, on the other hand, have been described as charitable or social organisations that embrace business systems. They might achieve this by simply importing management structures or a business culture without trying to understand or incorporate business principles in the way they work. My definition of social business is both deeper and broader. Social business is about using market values: identifying a problem, understanding the costs and the benefits of both the problem and the solution, and selling the benefits at a greater value than the costs. If you can get that mix right, and there is a profit margin, entrepreneurs will come in and fill that market gap. The problem will be addressed and eventually solved. When entrepreneurs or businesses use market forces to deliver goals of social or environmental change, that is social business.

If fundamental and lasting change is to occur in the areas traditionally occupied by charities it will be done within the structure and dynamics of markets. Charity will always be a marginal activity; it will have to badger, beg or borrow in order to survive and further its agenda.

Charities may argue that a for-profit model is not appropriate when you're trying to achieve something as vital and as altruistic as the eradication of AIDS. But I believe packaging the solution to a particular problem as a product or a service and then offering it to consumers is the most efficient way to effect change.

The best model for social enterprise is a for-profit model because it allows risk, growth and activity on a large scale. It also allows the founders of the enterprise to drive ahead without being slowed down by a board that's either concerned with its fiduciary responsibility to a charity's assets or focused on a purely financial return. Hopefully, boards that are comfortable in dealing with much higher levels of complexity will be the norm for both business and welfare organisations in the not-too-distant future.

There are signs that this is happening already. In June 2007, current affairs program *PM*, on the Australian Broadcasting Corporation's Radio National, ran a story about a charity deciding to branch into business to improve its chances of survival. The charity was Diabetes Australia–New South Wales (NSW), and it had announced it would take over the running of the state's Corporate Games, a sporting competition for teams of businesspeople. Diabetes Australia is dedicated to supporting people with diabetes, promoting education about the disease, and funding research into a cure. In the past, like most charities, Diabetes Australia–NSW had relied largely on donations and fund-raising events to finance its activities.

The radio story was framed by commentary implying that Diabetes Australia's decision to take this step was a reflection of how selfish our society had become; charities were being forced into business to survive. Despite our apparent affluence, the reporter said in concerned tones, it seems we're just too greedy to give to the less fortunate. I could almost see him shaking his head in disappointment at our collective stinginess; if only we all gave more to charity, he implied, everything would be perfect.

Prefaced in this manner, the story failed to highlight the positives of this development. This was actually a good news story. Here was a charity using lateral thinking to ensure it could continue to lobby for the people it had been set up to help by running a commercial enterprise that was consistent with its aims—maintaining health through being active. By combining its need to stay financially viable with commercial activity that was in perfect accord with its very reason for existing, Diabetes Australia–NSW is evolving into just the sort of enterprise this book is advocating. I take enormous encouragement from the fact that more charitable organisations are moving towards this model. If they take the kinds of initiatives that Diabetes Australia has, I have no doubt their objectives will be achieved sooner.

Occupying the middle space: for-profit, privately owned companies

The transition from a small-to-medium organisation built around an innovative and sometimes radical ideal to a large, established corporation is not easy, and early energy and purpose can be lost as organisations expand and consolidate. The founder of the Brotherhood of St Laurence, Father Gerard Tucker, was a man of tremendous energy and a true entrepreneur. His willingness to take risks and his legendary ability to bring about social change were lost to the Brotherhood over the years after his death. Anxious to safeguard its legend, its privileged position and the assets it had built up, the Brotherhood became risk-averse and conservative. It is not alone: many welfare organisations share this tendency to become more cautious and less nimble as they grow.

Ford Motor Company and the Bosch Group

The Ford Motor Company and the Bosch Group are two interesting examples of companies that essentially began as social-purpose businesses and have since become huge global enterprises. Henry Ford recognised that the people of a country as vast as the US would benefit from having a convenient way to stay in contact with their families. He was able to marry this social goal with his interest in things mechanical. He also implemented good business practices, including high wages (for the time) and shorter working hours for Ford employees.

While still a family-controlled business, Ford is now a publicly listed company that relies on manufacturing big, fossil-fuel-consuming cars. Over the last decade or so it has steadily been losing market share to Toyota, which has recognised that the market is changing and that consumers are looking for a range of cars, including more environmentally friendly vehicles. Toyota has been able to incorporate this social purpose—fuel-efficient cars—into its business model and in 2007 claimed a larger slice of the vehicle market than Ford.

Like Ford, at its inception in the late nineteenth century the Bosch Group, in addition to a commitment to high technology, assumed a socially responsible ethos. It has striven to continue this role, and the vast majority of the company's shares are owned by a charitable foundation, the Robert Bosch Foundation, which has no voting rights, while the management of the company, the Robert Bosch Industrial Trust KG, has almost all the voting rights but holds no shares.

The ownership and the management of Bosch are completely separate. Of the profits not ploughed back into the company, most go to the foundation for welfare projects. However, this separation means that the potential is there for the Bosch board to make decisions with negative social and environmental impacts and justify those decisions because it's making money for its shareholders. This is possible even though the major shareholder is a charitable foundation because the foundation doesn't manage the business.

Often, when a business becomes public it can lose its focus because its original concept and motivation is subsumed by the need to return a profit to the shareholders. A separation develops between the original strong social purpose and the perceived imperative to deliver ever-increasing profits. Inevitably, the social purpose is sacrificed.

As shareholders we have very little means to ensure a broader mix of considerations in the planning and decision-making processes of the companies we invest in. Social values are overwhelmed by profit concerns. Because of this lack of access investors, even the most socially conscious, tend to look at their pension funds only in terms of their financial return. The problem is sealed into the system.

Bill & Melinda Gates Foundation/Microsoft

Bill Gates, the founder of Microsoft, is an example of an entrepreneur who is using the wealth generated by his business to work towards a variety of social goals. Rather than doing this directly through his hugely successful company, this work is being done through the Bill & Melinda Gates Foundation, which is co-chaired by Bill Gates, his wife, Melinda, and his father, William Gates Snr. The foundation has an endowment of around $US30 billion and is funding sweeping programs for the control and eradication of diseases like malaria and AIDS and the reduction of poverty both in the US and globally. Microsoft, on the other hand, is a public company; it is managed by a board of directors (including Bill Gates) and is responsible to its shareholders.

The work of the Gates Foundation is obviously hugely significant and the work it does immensely important. However, I would argue that Bill Gates could make a much more profound impact on reducing poverty and disease by allowing free access globally to a common computer operating platform like Microsoft Windows. Making Windows freely available would give everyone in the world a much better chance to compete on an equal footing and to find and share information. Such a situation would be a great weapon in the fight against AIDS.

However, Gates couldn't make his products freely accessible, even if he wanted to. As the executive chairman of Microsoft, he is responsible to his shareholders and must provide ever-increasing dividends. Now, it's possible that he could argue for making all Microsoft products open source and demonstrate how the company could still continue to grow and perhaps generate even more profits. The Google model has shown that this approach can be extraordinarily successful. But it's not an easy task, and it would require a creative rethink of the whole Microsoft business strategy. It's much simpler for him to simply channel billions of dollars into a foundation committed to social goals.

Gates has created a disjunction for himself: as executive chairman of Microsoft he makes billions selling and licensing his products; as co-chairman of the Bill & Melinda Gates Foundation he steers what is probably the most far-reaching philanthropic project in history. And he's very successful in his latter role: he's very strategic and is able to tackle the foundation's various projects on a large scale simply because he has the financial resources to do that. However, this disjunction between his role at Microsoft, which is about exploiting and excluding, and his role in his foundation, which is about access and inclusion, means that in neither place is he working holistically. He is missing out on the integration that would allow Microsoft to effect social change in its very role as a successful commercial enterprise. I don't think the foundation, as remarkable as it is, delivers the same amount of change that it could if Gates changed his own business.

Google.com and Google.org

Google has created a similar separation between its commercial and its social goals with the creation of Google.org, its philanthropic arm. A much more open-source enterprise than Microsoft from its beginnings, Google has nonetheless grown into a ruthlessly commercial business. Google.org was started to support worthy causes without conflict with Google's obligations to shareholders. Much of the assistance it provides is in the form of access to the resources of Google.com.

While Google.org is very well resourced in financial terms, it's not keeping pace with Google.com. It seems to me that the reason for this is that it lacks the same willing-ness to take risks because it is hampered by the charity mindset. Rather than making the kinds of decisions that have made Google.com a world leader in search engines, Google.org has become bound up in 'doing good'. The entrepreneurial spirit that drives Google.com has yet to be established at Google.org.

The linkage between Google.org's good works and the Google.com product makes Google's arrangement, in my opinion, superior to the Gates model. However, the separation inhibits both arms from achieving their full potential. Rather than maintaining two separate entities, what would happen if Google asked itself, 'What are the twenty-five things we could do this year that will make the most money? What are the twenty-five things we could do that would do most to reduce global poverty? Are there five things that appear on both lists? Could we take a little less profit and dump Google.org but create stunning fundamental change in terms of our philanthropic goals? Could those poverty-reducing ventures be run in a profitable way so that we can focus all our brilliance, all our skills and all our resources on getting that change?'

In 2006, as CEO of Easy Being Green, I approached Google about establishing a uniformly accepted, quality standard for calculating carbon footprints and offsets. Such a standard, the Green Leaf, could be used to verify and validate carbon trading, and my proposal incorporated a model that would allow the project to fund itself. The Google representative's response was, 'Why do that when Google could simply fund it right now?' That's the charity mindset I'm talking about: yes, Google.com could fund this project while Google continues to thrive, but what happens if Google collapses? The idea will simply die if it isn't set up to be self-sustaining and given the same entrepreneurial opportunities as a commercial enterprise.

If I had pitched the proposal in the guise of a commercial enterprise in partnership with Google.com, the response may have been very different. Rather than simply offering to fund the proposal, the Google.com executives may have considered questions such as whether a carbon-trading portal could operate profitably. Time and resources would have been given to developing the concept so it could be set up as a self-sustaining enterprise.

A carbon-trading standard using something like a Google portal would allow us to accurately measure the carbon being saved and traded by companies and individuals. If every time that site sent you to an appropriate carbon offset supplier a couple of cents were deducted from any deals that were done, the enterprise could operate commercially. This would enable it to evolve and improve, staying relevant and becoming profitable. In fact, eighteen months after I had pitched this idea to Google, eBay launched an online trading platform for carbon credits with a similar scheme.

Grameen Bank

Perhaps the best known social enterprise in the world is the Grameen Bank, established by Mohammad Yunus in Bangladesh. The Grameen Bank extends micro-credit to the poorest of the poor, without any requirement for collateral. These loans assist mainly women in setting up small businesses to lift them out of poverty. Grameen is a for-profit enterprise; it has to be, otherwise it would have no chance of remaining viable. If it relied on donations—charity—to keep it going, it would have collapsed long ago. It is a bank with a social goal—lifting people out of poverty—and yet it manages to return a profit. As a result it can grow, and it now has around five million borrowers.

A charity simply couldn't achieve what Yunus has with the Grameen Bank. By using market principles, he has provided more practical and long-lasting assistance to the destitute in Bangladesh than anyone else. He has been able to do this because he has not floated the bank and he has retained control of his board. He's been able to make decisions because although the Grameen board has fiduciary responsibility, Yunus has imbued it with an understanding of the complex value mix it needs to consider. As a result the Grameen Bank is perhaps the ideal social-purpose business, and Yunus is both an outstandingly successful banker and a Nobel Peace laureate. Now that's living value-centred market economics.

COMPLEXITY OF STRUCTURES/ DECISION MAKING

We live in a complex world in which our mortgages have to be paid, our kids need to be educated, and we'd like to go on holiday at least once a year. But we also want to know that the opportunities and standard of living we enjoy aren't robbing the others we share the planet with or the generations to come.

As individuals, we routinely make decisions by weighing up a complex mesh of financial, emotional, moral, ethical and practical considerations. My belief is that we need to extend this complexity into our institutions so they can better represent us and all of our interests.

Our organisations, however, don't have sufficiently well-developed structures to manage complexity of the order that we deal with in our personal lives. At an enterprise level, we need to develop both the structures and the language to articulate and deliver a more complex mix of values. This will require change not only in the organisational structure but also in our psychology—the way we evaluate and make business decisions.

Rather than compartmentalising our lives, we need to let our decisions flow between our personal values, the way we run our businesses, the choices we make when we elect our leaders—once again, it's this idea of spirited sustainability. It is much simpler to keep each area of our lives separate and make decisions accordingly, but ultimately it is unsustainable on all levels.

The challenge for social entrepreneurs is to deliver the mix of social and other goals they want in a market-driven economy. The process will have to be more complex than in a purely for-profit business or a charity with no imperative to operate profitably. It is possible to have directors and boards who understand such a mix, but this sector is only new and they are far and few between.

If you really want to drive change, you've got to be in the real world—by engaging and operating within society, the market and the economy. Neither charity nor pure for-profit enterprises truly operate in the real world, because none of us make decisions purely on financial consider-ations or altruism alone. Social business provides a model of a middle space where the founders of the business can decide how they will pursue and achieve their goals.

Bridging the gap: Gerhardt Pearson of the Balkanu Cape York Development Corporation

The lives of many Aboriginal Australians, particularly those in remote communities, are characterised by a raft of afflic-tions including substandard living conditions; lack of services and employment opportunities; increased rates of incarceration, suicide and infant mortality; substance abuse and lower life expectancy. Successive governments have tried various approaches to improve the lives of Aboriginal Australians, and while there have been some success stories at both individual and community levels, failure has been the more common experience. Decades of welfare have failed to alleviate the problems, and some Aboriginal leaders have identified the culture of dependency as being at their root.

Can social enterprise be used to improve the lives of Aboriginal Australians and other disadvantaged communi-ties relying on welfare? How can the transition from welfare to economic independence be managed?

Gerhardt Pearson, executive director of the Balkanu Cape York Development Corporation, has wrestled with these questions and believes economic engagement is the key to transforming Aboriginal communities. Established in 1996 in far north Queensland, Balkanu works to support and develop enterprises that will allow Aboriginal people to engage in the mainstream economy. Gerhardt's brother, Noel Pearson, is the director of the Cape York Institute for Policy and Leadership, which develops policy on indigenous economic and welfare issues and fosters indigenous leaders in the Cape York area.

In their early years, Gerhardt and Noel's community of Hopevale in Cape York was run by the Lutheran Church. They witnessed the introduction of government welfare in the 1970s, and in the 1980s they fought for the right of the community to administer itself. Since then they have striven to develop and support opportunities for economic engagement in Cape York.

When Gerhardt was a child, his family grew their own fruit and vegetables, farmed pigs and chickens for meat and eggs and hunted and gathered bush tucker. The Church also provided rations of goods such as tobacco, tea, sugar and flour, and paid low wages to Gerhardt's parents for labour they performed in the community. The occasional tourist bus injected small amounts of money from outside. This situation changed with the introduction of welfare; as people's need for economic engagement was undermined, Gerhardt saw the vegetable gardens gradually fall into neglect and grog begin to take hold.

Not long after leaving school, Gerhardt spent several years living and working in Victoria. He returned to Hopevale and began working as the clerk for the Aboriginal council. When the council took over the administration of the community from the Church, it was now empowered to administer the funding the government provided for housing. Gerhardt saw an opportunity to use this money to grow local industry. He approached a local builder, with whom he already had a relationship, to develop a construction team that would employ and train people from the community. Because of this initiative, Hopevale now has indigenous people trained in all aspects of the building trade.

The Church had subsidised small community businesses such as the sawmill, but abandoned them when the Aboriginal council took over their administration. The businesses, built around the subsidies, began to collapse and the community lacked the business skills needed to reorganise them. Gerhardt secured grants from the Aboriginal Development Commission to ensure the survival of the businesses, accepting them with the proviso that people from the community be trained in their administration.

When the federal government agreed to a massive investment to provide sewerage, water and sealed roads in Hopevale, the Aboriginal council again explored ways to leverage business opportunities out of the situation. The council helped individuals to gain access to trucks, backhoes and other machinery so they could cart gravel and perform other paid work necessary for the implementation of these services. Such initiatives as these can form the basis of a transition strategy from welfare to enterprise.

In 1996, the Balkanu Cape York Development Corporation was established to support the creation of viable, sustainable businesses in the Cape. Gerhardt was appointed CEO, with two staff to assist him. Some twelve years later, Balkanu employs sixty-five people, and owns a fishing company and a broadband network that bring in revenue. It has supported indigenous people into business in a range of roles from tour guides to cleaners, rock musicians and earth movers. Balkanu has also developed

alliances with other organisations such as businesses—
including Westpac and the Boston Consulting Group—
universities and non-government organisations. These
partnerships bring expertise, mentoring and resources to
the Cape.

Gerhardt believes that meaningful economic engagement is the key not only to Aboriginal communities'
well-being but also to the larger agenda of reconciliation
with white Australians. Business development, he says,
creates opportunities for human transactions, not merely
financial ones. In driving these sorts of changes and
building enterprises and economic opportunities for the
indigenous people of the Cape, it is those in the business
sector, Gerhardt says, who understand best what Balkanu is
trying to achieve. He says:

> I've found an engagement with the corporates just
> down the road here [in Collins Street, Melbourne].
> They were in the dark about Aboriginal affairs; in
> many ways they'd ignored it. So when we broke the
> ice and got to know each other, the corporates
> realised that, 'We're in a position where we don't
> know what the solutions are. We've got to listen. What
> we have got is the know-how in terms of building
> enterprise, we've got the resources.' So they're offering
> resources, not solutions, which in many ways is the
> opposite of what government and the welfare bureau-
> cracy do. And I thought, 'We can get along here.'
>
> For example, we might ask the Boston Consulting
> Group to help someone—Willy Gordon—who has a
> little business that allows whitefellas to experience
> real Aboriginal culture. How can they help him
> develop his business? These consultants from

Melbourne visit Willy and see him directly engaging with whitefellas who are his paying customers. Those whitefellas, his customers and the corporate people, go away impressed by what they have seen, and by Willy, the individual. And it's at that point—that interaction—where there is the greatest point for achieving reconciliation. You never get that from a government-run forum where you have a bunch of whitefellas and blackfellas getting together in a place like this [an upmarket hotel in Melbourne]. It's too bland. But this business operation of Willy Gordon's, on his country, is a place where a real relationship can develop. They go away thinking, 'I didn't know black-fellas were like this. This guy has taught me a lot of things. I want to come back; I want to tell more people about it.' You know what I mean? Perception changes.

Selling peace: Jeremy Gilley and Peace One Day

No one would deny that war, on any number of levels, costs the communities and countries it is waged in dearly. Plenty of people have made money out of wars. But is it possible to create a business out of promoting peace and is it even appropriate to talk about peace as a commodity? As a social entrepreneur, it is exciting and sometimes challenging to see the partnerships formed between unlikely participants to promote social values (in this case, peace) in surprising ways.

Jeremy Gilley is the founder and sole owner of Peace One Day, a non-profit organisation dedicated to engaging all sectors of global society in recognising and participating in the United Nations International Day of Peace. Peace

One Day is a social business and does not have charity status. It funds its activities through a range of ventures including its annual flagship concert (in 2007 held at London's Royal Albert Hall); having its logo associated with brands such as Coca-Cola and Ecover (a manufacturer of ecological detergents and cleaning products); selling merchandise like Stella McCartney–designed T shirts; and using film, music, fashion, technology, education and celebrity to further its aims.

Peace One Day began in 1999 as a film project. Jeremy, an actor and film-maker, was looking for a way to address some of the issues he was becoming increasingly concerned about including persistent war, world hunger and environmental destruction. He became aware that there was no fixed calendar date for an international day of peace and ceasefire and decided to campaign for the establishment of such a day. In order to gain support and momentum for the project, he set about lobbying world leaders, including the then UN Secretary General, Kofi Annan, former Irish President Mary Robinson, His Holiness the Dalai Lama, the Secretary General of the League of Arab States, Amre Moussa, and several Nobel Peace laureates, filming his journey as he went.

In 2001, Jeremy achieved his initial objective: the UN General Assembly unanimously adopted a resolution put forward by the UK and Costa Rican governments to formally establish a global day of ceasefire and non-violence on 21 September every year—Peace Day. Jeremy had also made an award-winning film about the process of establishing the day, which provided the springboard to develop and further his aims.

In order to continue promoting Peace Day and widening its observance, Jeremy needed to find an organisational model that was financially sustainable. He applied to the Charities of Great Britain to register Peace One Day as a charity. The commission ruled that the organisation did not meet the requirements for registration because of its lobbying activities.

Jeremy decided to set up Peace One Day as a non-profit company, with himself as the sole owner, holding 100 per cent of the shares. While Jeremy draws a salary from the company, any profits made are returned to Peace One Day.

Jeremy believes that it is essential to engage all sectors of the community—government, NGOs, business, community groups and individuals—to achieve change. He is unapologetic about his refusal to exclude anyone from the conversation of how to further the aim of creating a more peaceful world:

> There are those that say we shouldn't take money from companies like Coca-Cola. I think that's a ridiculous statement—it's the big corporations of this world that should be funding these efforts. I think we need to be in the room with those CEOs, I think we need to empower them and inspire them. I don't think we should be throwing stones at them. Every one of them that I've met is a decent human being who has a family that they care about, and they care about the world.
>
> No individual can give us enough to do the work that we're doing, and indeed doesn't want to give us enough. We've had a donate button on our website for a very long time. Millions of people have looked at that website but a tiny, tiny percentage have even pressed the donate button. In fact, my next film is about how we can penetrate the corporations of

this world to take this message to the people. Would the United Corporations be more powerful than the United Nations? Yes.

Determined to build on his initial success and to ensure that an annual Peace Day grows so that it is observed all around the world, Jeremy has also written a children's book about his journey to establish the day, put together a resource pack for secondary school students, and continues to make films promoting Peace Day. His second feature film, to be released in 2008, will document life-saving activities specific to Peace Day carried out by humanitarian organisations around the world, including food distribution and mass immunisations.

In 2007, around 100 million people around the globe observed Peace Day.

Jeremy is my younger brother.

Balkanu Cape York Development Corporation
balkanu.com.au

Cape York Institute for Policy and Leadership
cyi.org.au

Peace One Day
peaceoneday.org

4

The role of government in value-centred market economics

In Chapter 3, I wrote that there is a crucial role for government in valuing goods and services in a way that is consistent with our moral and social aspirations. Rather than simply judging a government on its record of managing economic affairs, I believe we should redefine government's role to include placing economic value on activities that support the common good and ensure a sustainable planet.

Apart from the usual economic rhetoric about increasing GDP, opportunities for enterprise, an increased standard of living, the generation of profits and so on, governments find any discussion of value-based activity very difficult. If the delivery of financial goals is your overarching strategy, it's very easy to order all other priorities and policies around that. You simply weigh all your decisions on the scale of their financial outcome. However, many of the great social innovations of the last 100 years, such as universal health care and education, public housing and large infrastructure projects, have been made by governments whose goals were broader than simply maximising the ability to earn or create a budget surplus.

As I outlined in the previous chapter, the role of government, particularly in the last thirty years, has been primarily to foster the conditions for economic growth. Such growth equals prosperity for citizens, who can then buy more of the goods and services we equate with a higher standard of living. The not-so-secret ingredient of capitalism's success is its seemingly limitless ability to grow and to develop new markets. Perhaps because of this very success, governments seem to have forgotten that they have the means and the responsibility to frame those markets for the common good. In the past, however, governments were not afraid to actively and explicitly do this.

In the aftermath of World War II, governments, particularly in Western Europe and the UK, drastically re-evaluated their role in shaping society. Recoiling from the turmoil of the war years, they embarked on social reforms including national health-care schemes, grants for returned servicemen, welfare programs for the unemployed, and public housing. The horrors of war, if nothing else, had given people a hunger for security and governments, particularly in the UK, strove to deliver it by developing the welfare state while maintaining the conditions in which free markets could flourish. One of the consequences was an economic boom—a boom driven by value-based market economics.

The unregulated market and social values

It is, of course, possible for businesses and entrepreneurs to set social goals for themselves and their enterprises without relying on government support or endorsement. Through entrepreneurial nous and commitment, numerous enterprises have flourished while promoting and creating value above and beyond the purely financial. Many use the social goals they deliver as marketing tools to give them a competitive edge. One strikingly successful example is The Body Shop, established by Anita Roddick in 1976 and now a global cosmetics company. The Body Shop brand is based on natural ingredients, honesty in advertising, ethical business practices and fair trade. Roddick sold The Body Shop to the French cosmetics company L'Oréal in 2006, but up until her death in 2007 was associated with the company she founded and continued to actively campaign for social responsibility and human rights.

However, for social values to flourish across the whole economy, not just in isolated pockets, the involvement and leadership of government is crucial. Governments, through their power to legislate, impose taxes and develop and implement policy, have an enormous role to play in shaping market conditions so products and services can be ascribed their true cost or value.

While it is possible for an unregulated market to deliver great social good, there have been many instances where companies have exploited social and environmental resources purely for the opportunity to return cash to their shareholders. Exxon Mobil, for example, one of the largest oil and gas companies in the world, has been accused of funding lobby groups and think tanks sceptical of global warming in an effort to undermine action on the issue. The company's record on environmental responsibility is also poor, especially its handling of the *Exxon Valdez* oil spill in Prince William Sound, Alaska, in 1989.

Other notable examples of exploitation and misinformation campaigns have taken place in the tobacco, mining and resources industries. Particularly in Third World countries, there have been many cases of multinational companies ruthlessly exploiting the land and the people. In recent years, communities in Papua New Guinea and elsewhere have fought long and hard against the excesses of mining giants. The Ok Tedi mine in the Star Mountains of PNG, for example, has been operating for over twenty years, and in that time tens of thousands of tonnes of tailings and waste rock were dumped into the river every day. Forests died back, copper levels in the river increased drastically and fish were contaminated, as was the soil which supports food gardens and plantations. Since the 1990s, local landowners have brought various legal actions against Ok Tedi Mining and BHP Billiton for compensation for the damage. The Ok Tedi mine is set to operate until 2012 and, allegedly, toxic waste continues to be dumped into the river.

Campaigns also regularly highlight the plight of workers in the clothing industry in countries such as Bangladesh and the Philippines, who produce high-priced fashion for pitifully low pay and in shocking working conditions. It is not only 'Third World' workers who are exploited, but also outworkers in First World countries, often migrants, who, because of poor English skills or visa restrictions, are vulnerable to unethical treatment by employers that may include poor pay, cramped working conditions and unsafe work practices.

As a result of publicity campaigns pointing out these abuses, consumers view the companies that they purchase such goods from with suspicion, doubting their commitment to our planet and the common good. Several well-known sportswear companies have had to actively counter adverse publicity linking them to factories that employ sweatshop labour. In Australia, the wood-chipping company Gunns has been under intense scrutiny for its activities in the Tasmanian forests and its heavy-handed approach in dealing with opponents. Yet we rely on such enterprises and the markets in which they operate for the goods we desire. In the end companies are only able to get away with such behaviour because we invest in them and we buy their products.

GOVERNMENTS SHAPING MARKETS IN AUSTRALIA

Governments of all political colours regularly manipulate markets for particular outcomes. It's just that generally, and increasingly, those outcomes have a financial focus. The most important portfolio in any government is not the environment, indigenous or migrant affairs, or education; invariably it's the Treasury or Exchequer.

An interesting example of government shaping markets is the Australian response to four-wheel-drive vehicles (4WDs). In the 1970s these vehicles weren't manufactured in Australia. When farmers clamoured for these vehicles, the government lowered tariffs on them. At this time, there was an import tax on cars of 15 per cent, but to make 4WDs affordable for farmers import tax for these off-road vehicles was reduced to 5 per cent.

The goals behind this policy were social as well as financial, and at the time it made perfect sense: Australia was a big country, many rural roads were substandard; national prosperity relied heavily on farmers, both for exports and to feed the population. It made economic and social sense to help them access the goods they needed to deliver their products.

One would struggle to see how anyone at the time could have disagreed with the policy, particularly when there was little knowledge about pollution and absolutely no awareness of greenhouse gas emissions. It was an extremely sensible policy steeped in values both economic and social.

However, thirty years later in Australia, we have a 4WD explosion. Many suburban households are using these large, fuel-inefficient vehicles as their main transport. Such vehicles still have an import duty of only 5 per cent, while regular cars have an import duty of 10 per cent. Despite the toll they take on roads because of their weight, and their costliness because of their fuel consumption, the government continues to subsidise their importation, and they now account for around 20 per cent of the passenger-vehicle market. Motivated to buy these vehicles by their perceived prestige and their romantic association with the outback, most owners never drive them off-road. Instead they crowd kerbsides at school drop-off time and ferry groceries, occasionally transporting their owners to the ski fields or to the beach via sealed roads.

While I was still the director of the Brotherhood of St Laurence, we lobbied both sides of the political spectrum to have this policy of subsidising 4WD ownership overturned. We were told by both the Labor and Liberal parties that, although the lower import duty cost the nation around $500 million a year, the use of 4WDs was so prevalent in all the major cities that neither party would consider removing the tax advantage for those vehicles. A clear case of value-centred market economics: only in this case the value is now to safeguard political support. The outcome was that more and more people were driving more-polluting cars that were also more likely to result in death and injury in an accident. To change that policy and redefine the values it embraced required leadership and a willingness to make the case to the electorate. Certainly in early 2000, when I was speaking to both major parties, there was no willingness to take that kind of action or leadership and the subsidy is still in place.

Governments need to stay flexible in terms of policy so they can adjust and manipulate any mechanisms they activate in order to further a particular value. Circumstances alter, and governments have to be able to react quickly when they do. This flexibility should be seen as a valuable attribute in a government, not a liability, as it is often portrayed. Otherwise policies can become frozen in justifications that have become irrelevant to the original goal. In the case of Australia's 4WD subsidies, a government began by setting up a market-based framework to deliver a social and financial outcome. However that outcome and the reasons for seeking it became warped over time. The value was lost; now it's actually a negative value that the government still holds on to because they've become wedded to it.

In another arena, the Australian government has shaped and fostered a market with very tangible positive outcomes for society at large. For almost sixty years the Pharmaceutical Benefits Scheme (PBS) has made prescribed medicines available to Australians at a significantly subsidised cost.

For all medicines listed under the PBS there is a ceiling on the cost to consumers, regardless of the drugs' actual cost. Those who hold a government concession card pay even less. This policy is based on the belief that all Australians, regardless of their wealth, ought to have access to medicines that help maintain their health. It's a clear framework that allows consumers to get those medicines at an affordable price, and at the same time allows drug companies to compete for the right to supply them.

Because of the very secure market for their products, drug companies have been among the world's highest-returning investments. Constant demand for quality pharmaceuticals provides drug companies with money to spend on research and development. This in turn ensures that quality products continue to be developed. At the same time a competitive pharmaceutical market has driven growth, opportunity, jobs and wealth for the shareholders of those businesses.

There is a view in some quarters that the pharmaceutical industry has been overly protected globally. Particular criticism has been made with respect to the patenting of drugs, which has prevented low-cost generics being made available to populations in less wealthy countries. The industry has also been accused of 'inventing' diseases to create an expanding market for their products. Recognising this failure highlights the importance of getting the market framework right so that it fosters a mix of desirable outcomes: the social good of healthy populations, a high level of innovation and productivity, and a reliable product at a cost governments and consumers can afford. However, the underlying principle remains; governments have a vital role to play in the creation of strong, vibrant markets that also embrace social values.

MORE RECENT TRENDS IN GOVERNMENT

Increasingly governments, whether socialist or capitalist in their persuasion, claim legitimacy predominantly in terms of their ability to manage national economies. All other goals—security, better education, accessible health services, efficient transport systems and, particularly in the last ten years because of the growth of the green movement, environmental protection and sustainability—are relegated to secondary rank at best.

These commitments express themselves in government hierarchies. The top job is that of President, Prime Minister or Premier, the next most coveted position is that of Treasurer, Chancellor of the Exchequer or Secretary of the Treasury, then follows the Minister for Foreign Affairs or another high-profile ministry like Health or Employment, depending on the perceived flow of status and influence. Until quite recently, the environment portfolio was for the unlucky or those considered junior players.

The environment is one area in which there has been quite substantial movement. In an increasing number of countries around the world, the environment portfolio is the portfolio of choice for aspiring leaders partly because, depending on where you are in the world, climate change and water scarcity represent the biggest challenges and so have a high public profile. Two recent examples include Malcolm Turnbull in Australia, and David Miliband in the UK, who went from being Environment Secretary to Foreign Secretary.

The hierarchy of ministries, and the desire of those who head them to consolidate and increase their influence and power within the government—to protect their patch— leads to the rigid defining of the range of their responsibilities and areas of influence. This is not always conducive to an efficient and holistic delivery of a government's agenda.

Policy silos

Most governments have a range of ministries responsible for specific goals. However, since governments' chief interest is in managing the economy, some of those goals will be completely at odds with each other. Each ministry will be given a budget to enable it to deliver on some of the government's election pledges. They'll be spending money and not generating it, which ultimately will put them at odds with Treasury. And when Treasury gets tough, the other ministries inevitably lose out.

How do we overcome government's seemingly irresistible tendency to silo policy issues, when this approach is so entrenched? One way is to shift the policy debate so that social values are at the core of government rather than the periphery. This means broadening the range of values that governments tend to focus on and articulating those values more clearly. Rather than simply staking everything on how they plan to manage the budget and increase GDP in isolation, governments need to demonstrate how they will manage GDP in a way that will deliver and encourage a whole range of values, from sustainable use of resources to adequate health care for the elderly.

This kind of approach calls for a much more integrated Cabinet and departmental structure, because as I mentioned earlier most policy areas intersect with a range of other policy areas. For example, decisions based on environmental concerns and factors will have an impact on job creation and vice versa. A sustainable approach would see these types of decisions and their ramifications being assessed across government departments.

Britain's Performance and Innovation Unit

Increasingly, governments are recognising the pitfalls and limitations of the silo approach to policy. Not long after he became British Prime Minister, Tony Blair asked Geoff Mulgan, the then co-founder and director of the think tank Demos, to head up a cross-functional department. The Performance and Innovation Unit (PIU), as it was dubbed, was set up to integrate common values throughout central government departments. It was an attempt to break down the silo approach to government, where policy areas are strictly corralled and there is little communication between ministries on policy direction. It was an acknowl-edgement that an issue like employment had an impact on, and was affected by, policies in a range of areas such as welfare, law and order, immigration and border control, education and housing, among others. To achieve change on a significant issue such as this and to ensure a positive outcome, it was vital to try to coordinate and integrate the responses in all the various departments. This was a large part of the PIU's role.

In the late 1990s, a year or so into Tony Blair's first term in government, Geoff Mulgan brought the heads of four departments up to Liverpool to look over CREATE, one of the employment and training projects I was involved in. The group represented employment, social security, en-vironment and policing, and a meeting of such department heads would normally have occurred only in ministerial buildings. Apparently it was the first time that four depart-mental secretaries had ever been out of London to look at a case study together. That these four people had never met other than internally in a policy process was an indictment in itself.

Seeing an opportunity to challenge and perhaps influ-ence government policies that dictated the way CREATE had been delivering employment and training to the home-less, I opted for complete frankness. I explained to the secretaries that the only way we had achieved the success we had was by technically cheating the system. I say technically because while we were playing bureaucratic games, fudging grants and social security payments to give people mean- ingful work and training and to pay them, I believed we were delivering on the government's stated policy objectives in a way that was responsible in both economic and social terms.

'We are doing something that's extraordinarily successful for unemployed people,' I told them. 'We're generating jobs, paying fair wages and having a positive impact on the environment. We're doing all this and it is costing the government no more, but we have to cheat the system to make it happen.'

My question to them was: together, could they shift the system so the scheme we had developed and implemented could be legitimately replicated across the country?

Their response was overwhelmingly positive, and I watched them go with a sense of optimism: maybe, just maybe, those four departments could coordinate their policy to make our job of delivering employment and training easier. Some weeks later I received a lovely letter from the social security head praising our project and the work we had done. She really understood the challenge ahead for the government, she wrote, but unfortunately she didn't think her department could do anything to change the structures we were having to tap dance around. She suggested we just keep delivering our program in the same way.

Government silos were so entrenched that even these well-meaning and ostensibly powerful people were unable to see a way around them. The answer to my question had been an emphatic no. Even with a tailor-made agency to help them integrate values, the bureaucracy was simply not flexible enough.

The European Regional Development Fund

A more successful model for funding projects that span several policy areas has been implemented by the European Union. The European Regional Development Fund was established to support communities in poverty by promoting economic and social development. The fund had a very effective way of working across the various policy areas and departments of the EU. Regardless of which project was seeking funding, the applicants had to demonstrate the worth and sustainability of the project across a range of criteria—economic, social, financial, environmental. Whether the project was focused on job creation, training, housing or some other outcome, it was assessed on the values espoused by the EU as a whole, not just on the stated purpose of the project. To get funds, the project had to score a minimum number of points in each area.

I applied for funds from the ERDF when I was establishing the Furniture Resource Centre. It wasn't enough for me to show that I was providing training for the long-term unemployed; I had to prove that a market existed for recycled furniture and that the market was growing. I had to show how the FRC would generate income from the capital provided by the fund. It was a very innovative bureaucracy and it forced me to consider not only how I would retrain people but how that training would create jobs, opportunities and wealth for an impoverished community.

WHAT VCME MIGHT MEAN FOR GOVERNMENTS AND THE WAY WE VOTE

If voters began to see it as part of government's role to create the framework for value-centred market economics, the ramifications would be far-reaching. Currently, when Western governments undertake to provide services and infrastructure, including roads and hospitals, police or care for the elderly and unemployed, they expect to do so with taxes generated from free markets. If they shaped markets so as to deliver not just financial but social and environmental goals, they would need to describe their priorities in a much more far-reaching and cohesive way. They would need to provide a direction and a vision for the whole country.

A current example of governments taking this kind of approach has been motivated by climate change. As part of their commitment to the Kyoto Protocol, signatory nations agreed to create a market mechanism to encourage companies and governments to limit carbon dioxide emissions.

The US and Australia (prior to the election of the Rudd Labor government) notably refused to ratify the protocol. Both nations were unwilling to hamper business with the responsibility of protecting the environment. Instead they have opted for the competitive advantage of not imposing a carbon tax even when other countries have adopted this course. It's not difficult to see why they have taken this approach—both have large deposits of fossil fuels. Australia, especially, has a huge investment in continuing to mine and burn its deposits of high-polluting brown coal.

While other Western countries were ratifying Kyoto, the Howard-led Australian government effectively stated that it valued GDP above the environment. With the promise of economic prosperity and a higher standard of living, it attempted to bribe voters to accept this stand. However, in doing so it wilfully ignored the inevitable economic cost of global warming and continuing degradation of the ecosystem.

As global warming and climate change became greater considerations for voters, both sides of politics began taking the issue more seriously—though the Labor Party was marginally more willing to engage with the issue, promising to ratify Kyoto. Instead of playing catch-up with voters, it would have been heartening to see Australia's political elite showing leadership on this issue before it became politically expedient to do so.

In the lead-up to the 2007 Australian federal election, Labor finally showed the leadership demanded by the public and made climate change a defining message of its campaign. They won government and ratifying the Kyoto Agreement was one of its first political acts.

What might be the result of a government commitment to the future health of our planet? How would creating market mechanisms that factored in the true cost of carbon emissions have affected Australia's economic and industrial landscape? We might have seen the country emerge as a world leader, with a competitive edge in sustainable and non-polluting power industries. Investment in solar, wind, hydro and geothermal power could have vaulted Australia into a renewable-energy culture. Instead it maintained the advantages enjoyed by the fossil-fuel industries and intensifed the effects of climate change. It will be interesting to see how things change in the coming years.

It's true that a commitment to fossil fuels has meant some investment in useful technologies like carbon sequestration.

However, this was motivated not by the goal of caring for the planet, but to enable the exploitation of high-polluting resources to continue. It would be fantastic to see political parties creating a suite of policies aimed at delivering not just financial but social and environmental goals. As voters we must demand that our political parties articulate such overarching value goals. It would be a big change from the status quo, in which parties stress their handling of the economy above all else. As it is, environmental policies like investing in nuclear power or funding research on carbon sequestration do nothing to alter the factors that allow the problem to continue.

In order to move towards value-centred market economics, governments must consider new ways to engage voters. Rather than staking their claim to leadership on how they plan to manage the budget, politicians need to articulate their animating social values in a way that will capture the electorate's imagination and invite it to examine its own values. This may be a lot to ask, but I think all of us are frustrated with the paucity of options and lack of vision that are being presented to us.

CLIMATE CHANGE—AN EXAMPLE OF HOW GOVERNMENTS CAN ACT

The two most effective ways governments could reduce carbon emissions and alleviate climate change would be to remove all fuel subsidies and put a price on carbon. This would allow wind, solar and other green alternatives to compete. Instead of being at a premium, green energy would become the cheapest option.

Currently we're subsidising the cost of coal because we haven't looked at the full range of costs of burning it to provide electricity. The true costs include damage to the environment; worsening rates of diseases such as asthma; and the loss of potential new industries because of insufficient investment in green energy technology. We think coal is the only option: there are lots of coal mines and a strong lobby group with an interest in coal-fired electricity generation. We've become mired in that mindset.

Energy efficiency has a real role to play in reducing greenhouse gases, yet governments are hesitant to mandate change in this area. Yet we could achieve substantial improvement in energy efficiency if the law required, for example, that anyone buying a house that lacked energy-efficient fittings would have to install them. In Australia, this might add $5000 to the purchase price of an average home, but for a family of four or five such installations would save between $400 and $500 a year. Given that around 70 per cent of Australian houses change hands every six to seven years, that requirement alone would wipe out any future increase in household fuel demand and obliterate the need for any new coal-fired power stations.

Such shifts may well create negative consequences for some enterprises and individuals, but they would also create new markets, which business would step in to fill. Suddenly, there would be a huge demand for products and services that delivered energy efficiency. Guaranteed a market, industry would invest in research and development, jobs would be created and opportunities would emerge for exporting products and technology. But for such scenarios to develop, governments need to place economic value on activity that supports the common good.

The sphere that I operate in is that of carbon emissions and climate change, but there is no reason such a value-centred approach can't be applied to homelessness, education or social disadvantage. This approach is exemplified in examples like the Grameen Bank's offering micro-credit to the poor in Bangladesh, the Pearson brothers' work in creating business opportunities for indigenous people in Cape York, and Diabetes Australia–NSW's running a sporting competition.

Policy silos and climate change

Government projects and policies need to be assessed across a whole range of goals, not just one. With regard to climate change, a case in point is a carbon trading scheme my then company, Easy Being Green, participated in. Easy Being Green supplied energy-efficient shower heads and light bulbs free of charge to households across the Australian state of New South Wales (NSW). Because the shower heads reduced consumption of hot water, they also reduced power use and carbon dioxide emissions for each household. In return for the light bulbs and shower heads, we asked that these households sign over the carbon savings to us. We were able to sell these savings to energy providers, allowing them to avoid fines for excessive carbon production.

Now, a gas hot water system will heat water more efficiently than an electric one, and so produce less carbon dioxide. So while it was profitable for us to provide low-flow shower heads to households with an electric water heater in return for their carbon savings, it was not profitable for us to do the same deal for those households with gas hot water because their carbon emissions were already substantially less. The revenue we were able to generate from them was not enough to cover the cost of a shower head.

In addition to reducing a household's power use, though, an energy-efficient shower head reduces the water consumption of an average family by around 40,000 litres a year. The water board was also spending large sums providing households with efficient shower heads, not to reduce carbon emissions but to save water. Easy Being Green offered to take over the scheme in exchange for the cost of the shower heads, since we were already operating in this area and giving out the same product.

By any criteria—fiscal, efficiency, delivery of outcome—the adoption of our offer made sense. However, because we were trying to coordinate with two different government departments, two different ministers, we didn't have a chance. We could not reach an agreement. Instead of saving huge sums of money getting the product to households more quickly and efficiently, the impenetrable silos of government departments and the resulting barriers to communication and cooperation prevented the uptake of our offer—even though it embodied the goals the state government had expressly outlined in two key areas: water management and carbon-emissions reduction. The government instead relied on a raft of measures to achieve the very outcome Easy Being Green could have helped it deliver more cost effectively and efficiently. Governments must recognise the limits of the silo approach to policy development and implementation and force their ministers to develop more wide-reaching strategies.

RESPONSE OF THE SOCIAL ENTREPRENEUR

So what's the role of the social entrepreneur in the face of government's failure to provide the right mechanisms to deliver the goals it has articulated, or that it has not articulated but which still drive its decision making? In my view, it is to find creative ways around the barriers thrown up by bureaucracy and conflicting policies so as to achieve the outcome government really wants. It is then necessary to make a further leap and implement those solutions across the board so the impact of the innovation is not limited to a small, one-off project. This is true for both civic entrepreneurs (social entrepreneurs operating within government) and those working outside government.

For civic entrepreneurs, it's obviously vital to understand the value goals government is trying to achieve and then to smooth the way for NGOs or businesses whose activities are in harmony with those values. This may mean manipulating the rules from the inside to allow those outside to meet those goals. Clearly it's a risky strategy for the civic entrepreneur. In my working life I have probably met only one government bureaucrat who was willing to risk his job, on an almost daily basis, to achieve the outcome that he was employed to deliver. Most bureaucrats are by nature risk averse and assume their job is to protect their department head rather than open the gates to facilitate the department's goals. The security of bureaucracy is seductive and militates against risk.

The value of social entrepreneurs lies much less in the goods and services they provide than in the catalytic role they play in triggering innovations in the social sector. Like the business innovators who come up with major innovations for the marketplace, social entrepreneurs are the mad scientists, as it were—working away in their organisations that act like social innovation laboratories. They test and perfect different approaches, and when they come up with the most effective and efficient ones with the greatest impact it should be government and the corporate sectors' respective roles to celebrate the innovation, take it up, learn from it, and help scale it so that all can benefit. Ultimately, the innovation lies in the models devised for service and product delivery all along the supply chain— not in the provision of the good itself. It is those models that others need to take up and replicate.

Innovators in the public interest are the flame that ignites the fire of social transformation. That flame must be fanned and nurtured by governments, publicly traded and private companies, academia, media and individuals working together to achieve its promised impact.

Dr Pamela Hartigan, Managing Director, the Schwab Foundation for Social Entrepreneurship

It would be difficult to find a business that hasn't been frustrated by a bureaucracy even when it is trying to deliver a goal the government extols. Time and time again, schemes created to help business and NGOs deliver on government policy wind up in filing cabinets.

In 2007 when I was establishing my business Cool **nrg**, which seeks to implement energy efficiency globally, we had an opportunity to get funding from the Australian Trade Commission. The trouble was that by the time we stumbled upon this possibility, we had already begun to spend money in areas which, in some cases, made us ineligible to apply.

Bureaucracy shouldn't confine and corral government policy but actively seek out opportunities to implement it. If the bureaucracy is doing the former, then the role of the social entrepreneur is simply to persist and keep pushing. I have found that when trying to expand the opportunities for businesses to engage the issue of climate change, I've had to repeatedly tell bureaucrats, 'Your rhetoric is all about reducing greenhouse gases and cutting carbon emissions. My business is absolutely consistent with these goals, yet I'm receiving no assistance.'

Persistence is vital in my view, because I don't just want to grow a business on the back of climate change. I also want to see government action aligned with my business, because that's how I'll achieve my broader goals. In the Australian state of Victoria, Easy Being Green lobbied the government for three years to implement legislation that would allow us to trade carbon and thus push products into the market that would increase energy efficiency in households across the state. In April 2007, at the book launch of Murray Hogarth's *The 3rd Degree: Frontline in Australia's Climate War*, the Victorian environment minister said, very graciously, that the state's energy-efficiency targets, which create the opportunity for the market to deliver on climate change, existed because of the lobbying done by Easy Being Green. It was a rare acknowledgement from a government minister. The role of the social entrepreneur is to not give up on government but to press it to align its social goals with the market so we can all work together.

5
Business and values

The idea of value-centred market economics is thrown into stark relief in the arena of business. Ironically, perhaps, it's in the profit-focused corporate world where much of the discussion and work around values has occurred. Larger companies, particularly multinationals, give considerable prominence in their publicity material to notions of corporate responsibility to the community. This trend is also being picked up by medium-sized companies from hardware chains to pharmacies, which outline their value sets, not just their business goals.

This discussion is not only directed externally, to a company's potential partners, investors and customers, but internally towards its employees. It is in this area, the area of staffing, that business has directed a lot of energy into understanding the value sets employees hold and aspire to. The support of such values has, over the last ten years or so, been recognised by business as an important way to strengthen corporate culture and boost profits. Businesses increasingly use their commitment to sustainability, family friendly policies, volunteering and the like as recruitment tools.

So significant has been the work done in this area that a whole lexicon has emerged to express it: terms such as corporate social responsibility, triple bottom line, corporate citizenship and socially responsible business. All refer to broadening the criteria of success to include not just economic factors but also social or environmental ones.

Driving this expanded set of expectations for business has been the so-called 'stakeholder' movement. While previously businesses focused almost exclusively on customers, suppliers and shareholders, now they see themselves as playing to non-governmental organisations (NGOs) in the social and environmental arena, unions, increasingly demanding mainstream and values-based investors, corporate regulators, news media and employees.

Each of these groups has expectations for business that go beyond simple measures of financial performance to include environmental sustainability, social impact, transparent and fair corporate governance, and equitable workplace practices. A business able to make all these factors integral components of its operations, rather than add-on features of its marketing strategy, stands a better chance of satisfying the expectations of its diverse stakeholders and delivering on its business goals.

This is true particularly within large multinationals, and a range of rating and research systems has been developed to independently assess the capacity of companies to meet the demands of customers, employees, investors and various watchdogs. Increasingly, mainstream institutional investors view issues such as corporate governance, environmental performance and social impact as critical factors underpinning financial performance, and are requiring greater disclosure by companies of their systems for managing such issues and their performance in light of global best practices.

The degree to which terms such as corporate responsibility and triple bottom line are used in the media and within companies could make one think that the creation and communication of values has become embedded in business culture. If this is the case, then surely a conversation about value-centred market economics or value-centred market drivers, and their role in developing and sustaining profitability, would be readily understood. In fact, the use of the word value and its definition within business culture illustrate how little the business leopard has changed its spots.

Rather than developing a truly value-driven corporate culture, which would include leadership, innovation and staff happiness as well as profits, business has coopted the language of corporate social responsibility to allow it to continue to concentrate almost single-mindedly on the goal of maximising profits. Scant regard is actually given to creating the very values it espouses.

THE TRIPLE BOTTOM LINE AND CORPORATE SOCIAL RESPONSIBILITY

Business has recognised, at both the corporate and strategic level, the importance of communicating the broader concerns of the company, beyond its financial goals, to customers, staff and the broader community. Triple-bottom-line accounting and corporate social responsibility have become convenient terms that businesses use like flashcards to signal that they are responsible corporate citizens mindful of their obligations to both local and global communities and to the environment as well as their shareholders.

We have seen some very smart manoeuvres by companies that have allowed them to tinker around the edges of their methods of delivery, production and strategies, giving the impression of real engagement and commitment to a broad value base but actually doing little to change their recipe for profit generation. This small-scale change makes the companies more acceptable to consumers, but doesn't help them improve their core products or services.

McDonald's—an example

McDonald's, the takeaway food giant, was one of the first companies to identify the benefits of investing in the community in a significant and visible way. Ronald McDonald House Charities (RMHC) exists throughout the world, providing respite, support and accommodation for families of seriously ill children. While McDonald's doesn't own RMHC, being listed merely as one of its corporate partners, both are inextricably linked in the public's mind. McDonald's provides substantial support to RMHC in the way of free facilities, material and equipment and other costs. It also provides funds to the charity and holds fund-raising activities for it. The logo of RMHC also incorporates the image of the gloved hand of the Ronald McDonald clown, complete with the McDonald's golden M, holding a child's hand.

Many children's hospitals and the families of their patients, from Argentina to Hungary and from Brazil to Denmark, benefit from the Ronald McDonald houses. The houses mainly allow families to stay close to hospitals where children are being cared for. This set-up has proven to be a boon for hospitals and for families in need. It has also led McDonald's into relationships with the community that help it, as a business, learn how to deal with concerns about the company particularly regarding healthy eating and childhood obesity.

These concerns may be expressed in a general way by institutions or individuals, or in more direct attacks such as Morgan Spurlock's 2004 film *Super Size Me*. Over one month, the documentary film-maker ate only what he could buy at McDonald's and recorded the effects on his health. In response to the negative publicity the film brought, McDonald's stepped up its promotion of the 'healthier choices' it offers. Within a very short time after the film's release, McDonald's advertising began featuring these 'healthier' products and images of children engaged in physical activity. In Australia, McDonald's has gone so far as to submit these products, which include salads and the like, to the National Heart Foundation for assessment. The foundation has developed a standard (the Tick) to help consumers identify low-fat food choices. Products that meet the standard can display the Tick on their packaging. Several of McDonald's menu items did qualify for a Tick. It was a canny response by McDonald's, which rapidly adjusted to the concerns of the community with products and a marketing campaign to match.

The strategies McDonald's uses to combat negative perceptions of the company and its products were thrown into relief for me in February 2007, when my son, Charlie, who was eleven at the time, was admitted to hospital with appendicitis. It happened to be over the weekend, and as the hospital canteens were closed the closest and most convenient place to buy food was at McDonald's, which had an outlet inside the hospital. When I told Charlie I was going to leave him for a few minutes to get something to eat, he said, 'Dad, it's a bit strange isn't it, that the hospital lets McDonald's be here?' Even eleven-year-old Charlie, lying frightened and in pain in a hospital bed, could see the paradox of a fast food chain being embedded in a children's hospital.

Once in the restaurant and looking over the menu, I was struck by the fact that the 'lighter choices' menu items were significantly cheaper than the famous hamburgers. When I asked a staff member what the difference was between the chicken burger and the chicken roll (the healthier option), she replied that the roll had a bigger piece of chicken and more salad. It's clear that McDonald's is not expecting its 'lighter choices' menu to outsell its more traditional offerings any time soon. It fully expects the old chicken burger with chips, Big Macs and McNuggets to continue to generate most of its profits.

The importance of appearing to adopt a broader set of values has clearly not been lost on McDonald's, and obviously it is not alone in using such a marketing strategy. In the wider business community, a myriad of companies have two different value sets that they use to market themselves: one for investors and the other for customers. On the McDonald's website, you don't have to look very far to find the latter value set; much is made of the company's contribution to the community through its educational, environmental and sporting programs, its Corporation Social Responsibility Report and its focus on nutrition. Its annual report, however, is pretty much confined to an account of financial performance so McDonald's is under no illusion as to which information is of primary concern to its investors. Yes, Ronald McDonald House does provide real and welcome support to the families of sick children, and yes, a reasonably healthy meal can be purchased from a McDonald's restaurant, but these are not the drivers for the company; they are add-ons, mitigations to position themselves more positively in the marketplace.

While enormous effort globally has been put into improving the quality and relevance of sustainability or social reporting, some doubt remains as to the real changes to business operations and the values resulting from increased public disclosures. Reporting the extent of charitable support, the quality of environmental management systems and occupational health and safety standards can still be utterly divorced from the underlying nature of the business.

For all its 'lighter choice' food options and its association with children's health through RMHC, McDonald's has essentially kept its main business unchanged. It continues to sell standardised, high-fat food at an affordable price while its profits soar along with obesity and its cost to health.

LOCATING VALUE AT THE CENTRE

Is there a problem with the fact that some organisations have coopted certain social values to support a very narrow goal within their real mission, which may well run counter to the values that they are parading in their marketing?

I think there is a problem, and that's why social enterprise issues a useful challenge for those in business to consider. In contrast to many businesses, which tend to tack their social goals onto the edge of their core activity, social enterprise regards such values as a central or guiding principle. For social entrepreneurs, these goals are the first thing that we think about, the reason we go to work. They are not a marginal concern tacked on in self-justification after the rest of our business criteria have been fulfilled.

For me, personally, the values that imbue my business are not only what drive me, they also allow me to feel comfortable about how I live and the way I relate to my family and friends. Because I adhere to those values, there's no impediment to my getting very excited about the business itself and its potential for financial success. I get great pleasure from seeing the business grow and the share price increase; I'm intensely interested in the profit-and-loss statements and our profit margins. I grew up in an entrepreneurial family, and the game of business, the game of the market, is like food and drink to me. I'm also not immune to dreaming about what financial success could mean for me personally.

Despite all that, the social purpose of my business is my own purpose, the reason I have chosen this course. Primarily, I care about what I do and how I do it, not how much I stand to earn. I would not and could not work for a company that didn't let me feel proud about my contribution to the planet and to my family. If I weren't able to operate as a social entrepreneur—applying business principles to achieve a social and environmental outcome—no salary would be high enough to keep me in business; I would rather simply opt out of commerce, live in the country and build a house out of sustainable and recycled materials.

How can business respond?
For some companies, the conflict between the nature of their business and wider concerns of the community creates an extraordinary dilemma.

One of the biggest global issues we face is climate change. If your business is mining brown coal to be burnt in power stations to produce electricity, it is very difficult to shift your core activity easily. Yet, as concern grows about the social issue of global warming, if your business is to survive you must do something about that concern if you're to maintain your workforce and recruit new people. It may be necessary to offer a range of benefits and outline strategies and initiatives that will allow your employees to feel comfortable about their own role in a process they know is contributing to global warming.

So how could your hypothetical enterprise respond in business terms and still remain viable and relevant? One place to start would be to tell your staff and shareholders that you recognise the enormity of the problem that you are contributing to; that you realise the very nature of your business is a problem. Next step might be to inform them that you plan to strategically transition, not out of the business of generating power, but out of doing so in a way that produces massive amounts of carbon dioxide.

Once you embrace that idea and are committed to developing a strategy of change, you'll become known as a leading company committed to saving the planet. This requires a drastic change in priorities: suddenly the leader of the organisation becomes not the person responsible for digging the most coal out of the ground but the one defining a new energy strategy and a shift in the company's balance-sheet assets.

Perhaps that analysis seems simplistic, but a company that took on such a challenge at this moment would be delivering answers for every government in the world and establishing the path for every corporation to follow. The company that is in denial of the negative social impact of its business and is unwilling to change will be the company that fails. Such a company will present a risky proposition for shareholders, and those with an eye to the long term will start selling.

I want to make a play for companies to seriously consider what the more important values are; a consideration that in itself could generate an opportunity for them to lead, ethically and morally, but potentially also financially. Obviously this is not an insignificant challenge, and often the very leadership teams of large corporations are resistant to change. Overwhelmingly, the boards of most OECD companies are made up of the usual suspects. By that I mean white, middle-aged men. Occasionally a token white woman will be present, even more rarely someone from a non-English-speaking background. Any discussion will inevitably be limited if the members of a board have essentially the same life experiences. This situation is gradually beginning to change, but it remains true that most company board members are drawn from a very homogeneous group.

Changing the culture of a company so that a broader definition of value is embraced and striven for is not an easy task, but some companies are doing it and doing it very well. In Australia, one example that springs to mind is the Bendigo Bank, which has taken the lead in the community banking arena. It has captured a market segment abandoned by mainstream financial institutions by focusing on the needs of the communities in which it operates.

In the following chapter, I'll discuss other companies that are leading in the area of climate change.

I avoid working with governments wherever I can. I started out in the early 1970s working with international government agencies like the UN, OECD, USAID and so on, and learned a bunch of stuff along the way. But at the end of the year it was rarely possible to stand back and point to major outcomes as a result of all the effort. By contrast, working with business is much more satisfying, in the sense that you can see—have to see—results. If not, you're out on your neck.

For seven years through the 1990s I was a member of the European Commission's Consultative Forum on Environment & Sustainable Development, an experience that mainly confirmed my existing prejudices. But increasingly we will have to work out how to bridge the gap between the public, private and civil society sectors.

SustainAbility, in its first 20 years, has kept to its values by a combination of: being very clear what those values are; recruiting people who subscribe to them; being highly transparent in terms of who we are working with, what we are doing, and what works and what doesn't; and building first a Council and then a wider Faculty that help keep us on the right path.

John Elkington, Founder and Chief Entrepreneur, SustainAbility
A strategic management consultancy and think tank, SustainAbility advises clients on the risks and opportunities associated with corporate responsibility and sustainable development.

Leadership and the challenge for individuals

Over the past few years, I have been asked to speak about leadership in a considerable number of corporate organisations. Usually the CEO asks me to talk to their staff about how they might become more entrepreneurial and innovative, and how they might find, as individuals, the authority to speak their mind and begin to lead so the whole organisation becomes stronger and more energised.

Almost without exception, after delivering my talk, I walk away thinking if any employee actually did what I'd just suggested, they would severely limit their opportunities for advancement within that company. Big corporations, on the whole, are extremely conservative and resist any move away from a non-finance-driven direction. Most companies only know how to keep on doing what they've always done. They are happy to tinker around the edges in an effort to achieve improvements in the way they operate in response to changing circumstances or the latest thinking on various issues, but beyond that they would prefer to keep doing things the way they have always done them.

I am reminded of a talk that I gave a couple of years ago to the management and staff of one of Australia's leading car manufacturers. Outwardly, at least, this company is a leader in terms of its rhetoric about both its internal and external values. I was asked, as a progressive thinker on business and values, to come in and talk about leadership and innovation. In my talk I suggested that the company should create an environment where staff felt empowered to approach management with suggestions and comments that questioned the direction of the company—that asked if it was really looking to embrace the values of enterprise, leadership and innovation. Until staff had established that their position would still be secure if they expressed values and ideas that could be seen to be at odds with the company's, those values and the creativity that they required were unlikely to be seen in their workplace.

During my talk I posed several questions and asked for a show of hands in response. My first question was, 'How many of you feel that what you have to say is valued and that you have places to say it?' Hardly anyone put up their hand, except the boss and a couple of others. My next question was, 'How many of you see problems with the organisation but don't say anything?' Most of the staff put up their hand. 'How many of you believe that if you were to say those things it would jeopardise your job?' Again, most people put up their hand.

My challenge to those employees was to overcome that fear and find the courage to communicate honestly and openly with their bosses. In this way they would be honouring the values that were important to them, not just in their work but in their lives as a whole. In my experience, I told them, many bosses craved that kind of support, but all of us are much better at giving support to someone below than to someone higher up. Of course, there is an obvious reason for this: if you give support to someone above you and it's not accepted, you can lose your job!

The point I was trying to make was that the employees' own happiness was inextricably linked with the values of their workplace. They spent at least a third of their lives there, and if the values they implemented at work weren't consistent with those they strove for in other areas of their life, they were bound to be discontented. Choosing to work for a company whose values contradicted their own and refusing to challenge it tarred them with the same brush. However, if they did challenge the company on its values, they might well bring about the kind of company they wanted to work in.

Such a course is not without risk, but all of us need to take responsibility for the values espoused by our employers. If companies are using the rhetoric of value and innovation, then employees must call their bluff and act accordingly. In this way they can, through their engagement and honesty, help the company become the kind they would be proud to work in. Another possible outcome is that leadership of this kind could well be rewarded with promotion, increased salary and opportunities, and the pride that comes from knowing that you're standing up for what you believe in. Of course, the other possibility is discovering that your ideas and continued presence aren't required.

Leaving a job with no immediate prospects can be frightening. I have done it several times, knowing that I had responsibilities to my family, and I know it's not a light call to make. Sometimes, however, it's a necessary call. I have found that taking such risks always gives me a much clearer perspective on what I really want. Taking such a risk, I told the car manufacturer employees, even if the end result was the sack, would give them a strong starting place from which to find their next job.

In conversations with the staff after my talk, many told me that they found some of the ideas I raised inspiring and hopeful. I could also see that the challenge I had placed before them was probably not beyond some of the best in the company, but that it might be beyond the company's ability to respond.

The way forward

Business needs to embrace two distinct and yet related value sets if we are to meet the social and environmental crises that we face. One is the set of values that reflect the internal culture of the business: the workplace values in terms of staff. The other is the external values of the company: its social and environmental attitudes. Without an open, innovative culture and value set that has real impact on the way business operates, business can easily become a destructive rather than a productive component of society.

There is no fundamental conflict between the market and good social outcomes. Milton Friedman famously said the business of business is business, but I think a company's concern for the welfare of its community is sustainable business. Social entrepreneurs understand and embrace this. In today's society, one can be a capitalist and still behave in a way that is responsible to the planet and its citizens. Corporate Social Responsibility is not an oxymoron—it's a reality, and it's a way of conducting oneself that is becoming increasingly demanded by our stakeholders.

Marc Benioff, Founder and Chairman, Salesforce.com
Salesforce.com provides its clients with customer relationship management products and services. Committed to the idea that information technology can produce positive social change, Benioff created the Salesforce.com Foundation built around the 'one-percent model'. One per cent of company profits, equity and employee hours is given back to the community for projects including scholarships, renewable energy schemes and developing infrastructure for food distribution. Salesforce.com also supplies its product free for use by non-profit organisations.

Most corporate leaders understand that they will be rewarded in terms of customers and patronage if they are able to convey to the world that the value set of their company enhances the community and is environmentally and socially responsible. This in turn creates a strong, vibrant company with a profitable future. I have had this conversation many times with CEOs, and they nod their heads and agree, 'Yes, values are important.' I rarely see them able to respond in a way that actually changes their company's way of operating, particularly if it has been around longer than ten years. For that reason I believe the future of business, particularly in emerging industries like micro-credit, renewable energy and carbon trading, lies primarily with new companies that understand and aim for a more complex mix of values. These companies will be easily recognisable, and not just because of their social and community activities. The boards of these companies won't be made up solely of middle-aged white men, because the tasks they will be undertaking require a much more diverse range of people to run them.

In the chapter that follows, I talk about my experience creating a purpose-driven organisation.

6
Global warming: The changing conversation

I've chosen global warming as the main issue to discuss in terms of a social entrepreneurial response. This is not only because I have actively used my entrepreneurial skills over the last three years to develop a market response to climate change, but also because as somebody who's worked in the field of poverty for around twenty years, I believe global warming has the potential to create poverty on a scale bigger than we have ever faced.

For at least two decades, the world's leading environmental organisations and scientists have been talking about—and trying to engage politicians, business and the general public on—the issue of global warming. It has not been an easy task for several reasons, but I think there are two crucial ones. The first is that for a long time there was no consensus within the scientific community on the issue, and the second is that in the early stages of our awareness, it didn't appear that climate change would have an impact on the current, or even the next, generation. Given the relatively short-term cycles of politics and business, it was very difficult to further the discussion of an issue the effects of which, it appeared, would only be felt in the far distant future.

Of course, our understanding of the issue has now changed enormously. The effects of global warming are all around us, and while some politicians and business leaders refuse to see beyond their own short cycles of power and influence, the issue and its likely consequences for this generation and those to come have largely been grasped by the wider population.

GLOBAL WARMING AND SOCIAL ENTREPRENEURSHIP

Despite the activism of the Green movement over the last twenty years on environmental issues in general and in this particular area over the last five, and even with the recent conversion of many world leaders from global-warming sceptics to believers, we have still done little to reduce global greenhouse emissions. While there have been small efforts in this direction, far from declining, our carbon emissions are relentlessly increasing. A new and different response is required, and social business can help shape that response. For the past three years I have been working on growing a vibrant, sustainable business and providing secure employment for my staff while trying to deliver on the goal of reducing carbon emissions.

Before reflecting on how the issue has moved politically over the last few years, however, it's worth saying that the most significant aspect of the issue for me has been the response of individuals and our agreement or refusal to alter our familiar aspirations and habits. When I decided to go into the business of reducing greenhouse emissions, I believed that people wanted to act to solve the problem of global warming. I believed if I created a business that made it simple and cost effective for people to reduce their own emissions and save money at the same time, they would take up that option.

Disappointingly, what I've learnt is that while most people cite global warming as one of the most important issues facing humanity today, few do anything to reduce their own emissions. After five years of intense lobbying most of us simply do not consider relatively simple yet effective ways of reducing our carbon footprint, whether it be limiting car use or holiday air travel, buying energy-efficient light bulbs for our homes, or installing solar hot-water systems.

In most countries, less than two to three per cent of the light bulbs in people's homes are energy efficient. Even in a country like Australia, where solar hot water makes sense in both economic and environmental terms, a tiny proportion of homes and businesses have taken up this option. For two years I attempted to build a successful business based on the assumption that because people acknowledged the importance of the issue they would act on it. I learnt, to the business's detriment, that knowledge of an issue was not enough to change people's behaviour. I am now certain that because of short-sighted self-interest, the vast majority of people will only act to reduce their carbon emissions if the action is virtually taken for them or they are forced into it through legislation and other frameworks.

This realisation had a huge impact on the way I eventually chose to run my business. It also reminded me that as a social entrepreneur, my role is not simply to trust the market to deliver the values at the core of my business model, but also to demand that governments demonstrate their values through policies that allow a market that delivers social values to thrive.

My initial market response to global warming was the establishment of a company called Easy Being Green which, while I was writing this book, I followed with a second business, Cool **nrg**. Cool **nrg**'s goal is to build on the experience and lessons of Easy Being Green to launch a global business that will reduce carbon emissions. However, before looking at my entrepreneurial response, I believe it is worth exploring not the issue of climate change itself, but how the conversation around it has unfolded in the global consciousness.

THE EVOLUTION OF THE GLOBAL-WARMING DEBATE

Climate change as an issue has transformed, in a relatively short time, from a fanciful idea where to be a sceptic was the norm to a matter of global concern. Once, to advocate change in this area was to invite ridicule and to be dismissed as an over-reactive greenie. Now, sceptics are increasingly seen as irresponsible, with their heads in the sand. Global warming is discussed and examined on TV, on radio, in newspapers, books and magazines, in classrooms and in our conversations with family, friends and colleagues.

This change in perception will, I believe, result in a shift in values that will in turn bring a radical new suite of government leadership initiatives with the potential to create opportunities for the market to fall in and support these new values. Regardless of the motives of that market,

I believe that by engaging it we may be able to achieve significant reductions of carbon emissions and go some way toward averting what could well be a catastrophe for humanity.

Even now, with the dire predictions of where inaction on global warming could lead, to speak of catastrophe is still not acceptable in many circles. We are not ready to accept that level of alarm. Most of us, however, are convinced that global warming is a reality and are willing to consider the possibility of the loss of species like polar bears and natural phenomena like the Great Barrier Reef. We are not yet ready to consider that 100 million people in Bangladesh could become environmental refugees because of rising sea levels or that many of us who live near the coast, even those who feel protected by our relative wealth, could also lose our homes. Despite the general reluctance to accept this as a reality, this scenario is gaining credence. In 2007, in awarding the Nobel Peace Prize jointly to Al Gore and the Intergovernmental Panel on Climate Change, the Nobel committee expressly linked climate change with the potential for catastrophe because of large-scale migration and conflict over resources.

As somebody who was not working in the environmental field during the initial Kyoto conversations, I—like many people—viewed global warming as an important issue, but one that existed on the periphery of my life. I was unsurprised when both the US and Australia adopted a position based on self-interest and inaction, but I was grateful for the leadership of Europe.

It was shortly after Kyoto that I was recognised as a Schwab social entrepreneur and invited to attend the World Economic Forum. My first Forum was in New York in the January after the Twin Towers disaster of 9/11, and the meeting was dominated by issues of security. In the seven or so years since that event, I have been to four Forums and have witnessed the dramatic change in the way climate change and global warming has been dealt with.

At that first Forum in New York, there were some speakers addressing climate change and, when I wasn't busy with my own agenda of poverty, I began to pay attention to the subject. It became clear to me that this thing dubbed global warming was an important issue that was likely to have a significant impact in the longer term on poverty.

Not surprisingly, given the world we live in, and that the World Economic Forum is mainly attended by political and business leaders, most of its participants are men. However, many bring their wives and partners with them, and many of these women attend much of the conference. It quickly became apparent to me that while the sessions dealing with security or mainstream business issues were packed with men, the climate change and poverty sessions were dominated by their spouses. While male captains of industry and political leaders showed little interest, the wives of some of the most powerful men on the planet were steering and participating in the conversations on climate change and poverty, the 'peripheral' issues.

Nothing really changed to rock the boat or the focuses of the World Economic Forum until the January 2005 Forum. It was there that the British Prime Minister, Tony Blair, made a powerful speech on climate change. Bill Clinton, the former US President, also noted the importance of the issue.

At this time, I had recently established Easy Being Green and was therefore watching the issue very closely. Some players in the business sector had also begun to take a more than passing interest in climate change and were particularly keen to come to grips with how increasing carbon emissions might hurt their profits and their business strategies. Certainly some insurance companies and major banks were taking a lead; they were already beginning to see the trends emerging because of climate changes and the impact freak weather events could have on their businesses.

Still, with the exception of those businesses dealing with risk on a large scale, and some enlightened political leaders, the issue, particularly in terms of business and broader politics, was still dominated by the sceptics. In Australia and globally, many heavyweights of business, particularly those involved in the mining industry, began to stridently oppose any moves to deal with global warming on a large scale. They had the money, profile and influence to lobby governments with dire economic predictions if they moved to act on climate change. They also attempted to discredit scientists trying to raise awareness of the issue. They were determined that burning fossil fuels, and their businesses that relied on it, would not be adversely affected by the growing noise of the global warming debate. They had witnessed the impact on the tobacco industry that public awareness of the link between cancer and smoking had had, despite that industry's attempts to stifle such awareness.

Despite the opposition of powerful business interests, something had shifted in the climate change debate; a watershed had been reached. Blair and Clinton had made a call, backing the majority of scientific thinking with their considerable leadership and political credibility, and there were some business leaders who had come to engage constructively in the debate.

At the 2006 Forum, the sessions on climate change were harder to get into due to their increased popularity. At the plenary session, where participants rated the issues under discussion, climate change emerged as one of the major risk issues for the business world.

Two years later, the world had certainly moved on. At the January 2007 Forum in Davos, it was almost impossible to get a seat in any of the environment or climate change debates. Businesses from every sector had accepted global warming as a major risk issue and could see that its impact would be felt on their companies within the next ten, twenty or thirty years, for some even less. For the enlightened business leaders, global warming was shaping up not simply as a threat to business but also as having the potential to create new markets. Venture capitalists were sniffing around companies working in the renewable energy areas as if they held the promise of a new dot-com era.

Sessions that included Tony Blair, economist Nicholas Stern or any of the many climate-change leaders present were booked out the moment seats became available. Rather unfairly, the spouses who had participated in the earlier discussions on global warming were no longer able to attend—there simply wasn't room. The debate had been taken over by overweight, white, fifty-something businessmen. The issue had taken hold.

Economic opportunity

Why had there been such a dramatic shift? Partly it was a result of the Kyoto Protocol, which had been ratified by almost all UN member countries except, most notably, the US and Australia. A substantial market in carbon trading had been established in Europe worth billions of euros. Although the price was fluctuating and in 2006 had dropped considerably, the carbon market hadn't collapsed and has a strong future. Kyoto had created winners, losers and leaders in the global warming economy.

The winners on the whole were European companies that had engaged with the carbon market and were building new businesses around it. Within China, one of the biggest emitters of greenhouses gases, a whole stream of entrepreneurs and billionaires was emerging. In 2006, at least three launches of renewable-energy businesses have made a number of Chinese businessmen incredibly wealthy. The time for investing in businesses engaging with global warming had come.

As I mentioned, there were also losers in the wake of the Kyoto Protocol. Those countries that had not ratified the protocol found they had been accorded almost a pariah status. As an Australian at the WEF in 2007, it was impossible to ignore the way in which Australia was invariably mentioned in connection with the US as being part of the problem of inaction on climate change. Often the names of the two countries were rattled off together to give the effect of one nation: 'the Usandaustralia'.

Surprisingly enough, opportunities existed to lead even within those countries that elected not to sign on to Kyoto. In the Australian state of New South Wales a carbon trading market was created that was the second largest on the planet. The NSW government, under Premier Bob Carr, showed extraordinary leadership in the face of an Australian Federal Government reluctant even to believe global warming existed. It established a small independent trading market which my then company, Easy Being Green, in 2006 had been able to use to deliver one of the biggest campaigns ever to engage with individual home owners on reducing their carbon emissions.

The Kyoto Protocol is also about to come of age; in its 2008–2012 round it will, I believe, create a strong and vibrant global carbon market. This market will generate new businesses, new ideas, new opportunities and extra-ordinary wealth. Those of us living in countries without the benefit of a comprehensive government strategy to deal with global warming, will have to work harder to find the same opportunities. Despite Australia's recent commitment to ratify Kyoto, it is still a long way behind the now maturing markets in countries that ratified it earlier. Yet, almost paradoxically, because Australia was outside of Kyoto and therefore its trading platform, our opportunities to lead in this new market were still great.

In early 2007, the Australian Prime Minister, John Howard (a global warming sceptic), appointed a new Environment Minister who, within a month of starting his new job, committed to banning the sale of incandescent light bulbs, forcing all Australians within the next two years to buy compact fluorescent light bulbs. This one act of legislation meant that Australia was suddenly leading the world in progressive change on global warming. Similarly, the newly elected Prime Minister, Kevin Rudd, was hailed as a hero at the Bali climate change talks for changing Australian policy and leaving the US isolated.

Leadership

Despite Kyoto's impact, I don't believe it was the single factor that shifted thinking on this issue. There have, in fact, been several examples of leadership that have been crucial in furthering action on climate change. I'll mention a handful here, but there have been others.

For around fifteen years or so and particularly in the last five or six, petroleum giant BP, led by Lord Browne, has recognised the seriousness of global warming and acknowledged its role in it. The name change from British Petroleum to Beyond Petroleum, while having the potential to be seen merely as a token gesture, has allowed BP to consider the impact of its business and set itself up for change. In early 2007 it laid further claim to a leadership role in the climate-change area by offering carbon-neutral products and setting standards for carbon offsets.

Similarly, in 2005 the CEO of GE, the technology and services conglomerate, made a public commitment that by 2010 at least $20 billion of its revenue would be drawn from businesses that helped customers to improve their environmental impact. That kind of leadership at that point was quite exceptional.

In Australia, Insurance Australia Group (IAG), working with the World Wide Fund for Nature, established the Australian Climate Group (ACG). In July 2004, the ACG released information on climate change that IAG had gleaned through analysing insurance claims. That sharing of knowledge greatly advanced our understanding of the real impact on business of global change. Yet these companies—BP, IAG, GE—stand out among the vast majority of businesses, which proceed with scant regard for how their actions affect the earth.

In addition to these leaders in the commercial sector, Tony Blair's speech at the 2005 World Economic Forum and his championing of climate change as an issue during his presidency of the G8 helped to shift the thinking of other world leaders. Al Gore's release of his documentary *An Inconvenient Truth* in August 2006 was also a pivotal moment in establishing climate change as a global issue. As someone who had been within a whisker of becoming US President, Gore brought a credibility to the issue that caught the attention of many.

Two months after the release of *An Inconvenient Truth*, former World Bank Chief Economist Sir Nicholas Stern released his report on the economics of climate change. He predicted that if climate change was not addressed it would cost between 5 and 20 per cent of annual global GDP now and into the future. At the end of 2006, the Intergovernmental Panel on Climate Change's (IPCC) report stated that global warming was a direct consequence of our generation of carbon. Global warming was beginning to share the agenda of international discussions along with security and trade. At the G8 summit in Germany in 2007, it was announced that the member nations would 'aim to at least halve global carbon dioxide emissions by 2050'.

Leadership from these individuals and institutions was undoubtedly the turning point, but the groundwork for the corporate and political leadership that we now see was nevertheless laid by the campaigning of environmental organisations that, on the whole, had been marginalised and discredited for twenty years.

In Australia, prolonged drought, hot summers and a severe bushfire season in 2006–07 had brought the global issue well and truly home. In Europe and America, too, over the last few years, extreme weather conditions have brought hurricanes, drought, floods and deaths from heat exhaustion.

Suddenly there seemed to be a plethora of events and reports all pointing towards the severity of global warming and the consequences of inaction. The politics had moved, the scientific community had moved, and suddenly there was a united front calling for action.

In Australia, in February 2007, an unmistakable sign that the tide had turned came when Prime Minister John Howard had to return to the Parliament to correct an answer he had given to a question regarding climate change a few hours earlier. He had initially stated that 'the jury was out' when he was asked about the link between global warming and carbon emissions, but returned to say he accepted that such a link existed and had misheard the original question. Finally, politically, there was no space any longer to be a sceptic.

When John Howard and the Liberal Party lost the federal election in November 2007, many commentators attributed the loss to Howard's misreading of public sentiment on two issues. One was industrial relations, the other was climate change. As part of their election campaign, the Labor Party had pledged to ratify the Kyoto Protocol. They were swept into office and did sign Kyoto. Days after the election, the newly elected Liberal Party leader endorsed Labor's move.

MEDIA TREATMENT OF GLOBAL WARMING

During this time, when the conversation around global warming was evolving so rapidly, I found the media's treatment of the issue fascinating. As somebody who'd been trying to get this issue into the press for three years with little success, I was staggered by the sudden explosion of articles on this very topic. Initially, for every opinion piece calling for action on climate change there would be another expressing scepticism, if not of the theory, then of the severity of the likely consequences.

By late 2006, and especially after the release of the Stern Report, the media's treatment of the issue had changed. The debate had moved from a technical discussion to an emotive one. Suddenly the graphs representing the temperature of the ocean and fluctuating weather patterns over the last few decades were replaced by photographs of polar bears, Pacific islands and low-lying villages in Third World countries.

In a remarkable turnaround, in late 2006 Rupert Murdoch, previously a global warming sceptic, publicly announced that he accepted the threat of climate change and the likelihood that humanity's activities contributed to it. In May 2007 he went further, pledging that his corporation, News Corp, would be carbon neutral by 2010. At Cool **nrg** we have worked with many News Corp publications that had previously given a platform to those wishing to discredit climate change activists. On the whole this scepticism within News Corp has been replaced by a commitment to action and an engagement with climate change.

The media have finally embraced global warming as an issue to be campaigned on in terms of the future of the planet. It's in this context that one can truly say that there is now an opportunity to align the values of government in a way that could allow markets to work, operate and succeed, and therefore deliver change on this issue.

The issue of climate change and global warming has now gathered momentum to the extent that it can no longer be ignored (although in the US concern is still nowhere near as widespread as in the rest of the world). While there is a desire for carbon emissions reduction and other strategies to ameliorate the effects of global warming, there is confusion about how to achieve the necessary change. Social business and social entrepreneurs can provide models and solutions using existing market structures. Traditionally, commercial enterprises have not been concerned with delivering social or environmental change. Yet the market is the only mechanism that can deliver the scale of change needed at the pace required in this area. In the next chapter, I'll explore how this can happen.

7
VCME living and leadership

My response as a social entrepreneur to the issue of global warming hasn't followed a particularly linear or straightforward path. It has taken me through several different permutations of business models and structures and required me to readjust my focus a number of times. Although I have been working in the area of climate change for three years, it is only recently, I realise, that I have begun doing so in a truly socially entrepreneurial way.

When I started the company that preceded Cool **nrg**, Easy Being Green, I believed that a purely market-based effort—establishing a company selling affordable products that made it easy for people to act on their concerns about the environment—would be enough to make that business successful. What I hope will emerge in this story, in terms of the thinking behind value-centred market economics, is two things were needed to ensure success: a willingness in the market to explore products that delivered carbon emissions reductions and a strong legislative framework that supported the same objective.

As with the success we achieved with the Furniture Resource Centre, which required a legislative framework that shifted the cost of homelessness away from homeless people onto those agencies and enterprises that benefited from improving their support for them (primarily landlords and government agencies), success in a market-driven reduction of carbon emissions required similar support from government. It was not until government began to value emissions reduction and legislate to help achieve it that we saw a vibrant market response to the challenge. However, I say that with three years' worth of hindsight. In this chapter, I want to trace the journey that brought us to that point.

CHALLENGING MYSELF TO LEAD

Klaus Schwab, the founder of the World Economic Forum (WEF), created a framework to identify and recognise some of the world's leading social entrepreneurs. He wanted to bring them into the WEF to help businesspeople consider and work for goals beyond simply increasing earnings per share or creating capital.

I was very honoured to be one of the first thirty social entrepreneurs recognised by the Schwab Foundation while working at the Brotherhood of St Laurence. As the Brotherhood was already a well-established organisation, what I found most exciting about it was bringing to the WEF my fifteen years of experience as a social entrepreneur and my previous experience as a businessman without having to worry about advancing any particular agenda associated with the Brotherhood. I hoped to influence, where I could, the thinking of CEOs and other economic leaders about the role of leadership in business and encourage them to look for ways to serve bigger and broader social values as well as being profitable.

It was during this time that I realised I was going to the WEF in the hope that the other participants would tackle some of the social issues that I'd felt were beyond me as CEO of a relatively small welfare organisation. At the same time, I had begun to form the opinion that making inroads into the big, intractable issues like the environment, exploitation of the Third World, disease and malnutrition required the involvement of global organisations. For example, if Coca-Cola decided to take the caffeine out of Coke, that would achieve a much bigger public health benefit than a small, single-country campaign on the effects of caffeine on children. This is why it's imperative that corporations such as Coca-Cola are always revisited as potential 'value' partners, as recognised by Jeremy Gilley.

By the time I left the Brotherhood, I was absolutely convinced that change on a global scale called for the involvement of organisations of global scale, and that while I'd been prepared to challenge others to deliver change, I had kept myself and my own position quite safe.

The second conviction was the more profound in terms of the ramifications for me, personally. I had been calling on business leaders who were under pressure from bosses or boards or shareholders to deliver the sole value of more wealth, and I was expecting them to broaden that value base and to take the risks for the goals I believed in. I had been preaching, from a very safe position, that others under very powerful constraints should take that risk on my behalf, or on behalf of society. I came to realise that if I believed that I had a contribution to make and was a good leader and a good businessman, I had an obligation to take on the challenge myself.

Now, as I've said, I believe that leaders who take such risks and succeed in creating a broader value base for business are likely to be the leaders of the future, in the companies of the future. However, it's one thing to believe that and preach it and quite another to risk your own position and self-esteem to try and achieve it. By the time I decided to leave the Brotherhood, I had resolved that in my next role I would take on the same risks I had previously demanded of others. I began to consider exactly how I might bring about some of the social outcomes I believed in through the market and on a global scale.

I decided to leave the Brotherhood in part because I was not a great change manager. My previous successes had been in founding and leading organisations and teams. With the Brotherhood I found myself in a mature organisation with an entrenched culture. My colleagues were strongly resistant to change and I was surprised to find some prepared to actively undermine change. Once I fully understood the situation, I made up my mind to leave and began to think about what I might do next.

A characteristic shared by all of the social entrepreneurs I know is their empathy for others. They are not only visionaries but they have the strengths and capability to realise their dreams, with the strong conviction that what they do is beneficial for humankind.

Hilde Schwab, President and Co-Founder, Schwab Foundation for Social Entrepreneurship

THE THREADS THAT LED TO NEW BUSINESS

As a relatively recent immigrant, I began to consider ways that I might better engage with the Australian community.

The reasons I wanted to stay did not revolve around the beauty of the landscape, the relaxed lifestyle or the other commonly cited benefits of life in Australia, real though they might be. Neither were they based on opportunities that existed in Australia for piloting business innovations, be they in products, business models or marketing. These do exist because Australia has a small population yet much in common with the much larger nations of Europe and the US, so it's a great place to trial innovations and from which to export ideas and products. None of these realities was enough to serve as a bedrock on which to build a life in Australia. Apart from my family, I wanted to find a reason to stay in Australia that had integrity and honour.

My biggest reservation about remaining in Australia was that after five years in social services, I had become acutely aware of the plight of indigenous people. As a white person who enjoyed the privileges of being one of the majority, I felt a degree of culpability for the injustices that had been inflicted on the indigenous people for over two centuries and which still continued. I was, and still am, staggered that most Australians don't seem to acknowledge this or have the political will to address it. If I was to remain in Australia, I wanted to do so in a way that acknowledged indigenous people and their struggle.

It seemed to me that I had two options. The first was to continue to work in a similar role to the one I had held at the Brotherhood and apply market principles to ending indigenous disadvantage. Clearly, if there were ever a place where markets and government policy needed to come together, it was around indigenous affairs. However, I was reluctant to be yet another white consultant earning much more money than the indigenous people I worked alongside.

The second option had to do with the land itself. Australians, on a per capita basis, are the most wasteful consumers of water on the planet. We are also second only to Americans in our per capita production of carbon dioxide; it is no surprise that both our nations had refused to ratify the Kyoto Protocol. White people stole the land in Australia and, in my view, it is no coincidence that we abuse it. All of us are likely to feel a more profound connection with something we feel we belong to and that belongs to us. Indigenous Australians are spiritually and intimately connected to the land, so I thought that if I could work in a way that honoured the land that would be a worthwhile contribution. Working towards a sustainable use of Australia's land and resources and then applying what I learned to global change became my goal.

Another driver which actually gave me the idea for this new business was my exposure to the issues, raised in the World Economic Forum, particularly climate change. It was becoming clear to me that it was the biggest social issue on Earth. Not only would there be immediate effects of climate change, like more frequent and severe hurricanes and typhoons with resulting death and social destabilisation, but in the longer term Third World countries already struggling with poverty, disease and malnutrition would find their resources stretched even further. To continue to consider the short-term needs of people in poverty without addressing the potentially devastating global effects of climate change began to seem wilfully short-sighted.

As all these threads began to pull together—my desire to honour the land; the issue of global warming; using the market to achieve change on a global scale—the idea took shape of a business that would help the many people who recognised the importance of environmental issues to act to improve the energy and water efficiency in their homes.

With that idea in mind, and while I was serving out my twelve months' notice at the Brotherhood, I came up with the idea of a website that would give people the information they needed to choose energy- and water-efficient services or products and access them. I played with the idea for a couple of months and decided that if I was going to be serious about this, I needed time to explore it. To that end I decided to form a company, which in itself was an interesting process that got me to reflect on my values and how I might want to structure a business.

Despite having lived in Australia for six years, and on the cusp of launching a business, I realised I had few friends outside of my work. This was partly because I was a recent immigrant and my job as CEO of the Brotherhood was so demanding and partly because of the time commitments of having a young family. I decided that if I was going to create a new business, I would do it in a way that opened out my social life rather than shrinking it. My new business, whatever it became, would involve people I liked, people I respected, people who would help me build a broader value base in my life beyond work.

To that end, in mid-2003 I began to contact people whose company I'd enjoyed over the years, who had been helpful or supportive, and who I thought would be interested in setting up an environmental business. I approached about a dozen people I liked and invited them to join me in a three-month exploration of my idea. We began to meet fortnightly over pizza and wine to discuss and research the issues. We then tried to refine them into viable business concepts. It was agreed that each participant in these discussions would get one per cent of the business we set up. As a result of those discussions, we came up with the initial business model of Easy Being Green.

The twelve of us involved in those early discussions all shared a similar experience: while we wanted to do more personally to address environmental issues, we had found this difficult and expensive. It seemed to us that an opportunity existed for a business that could make it easier for more people to take action in this area. We did some research and were heartened to find that 80 to 90 per cent of Australians believed it was important to act individually on environmental issues. We also looked at many of the companies that were offering energy-saving and emissions-reducing products and found that in many cases they were not accessible or there was too little information about them. A company that made it easy and affordable for individuals to be green started to seem like a great idea.

In February 2004, two months after I left the Brotherhood of St Laurence, I and another member of our group, Chris Tierney, rented an office and officially launched the company.

EARLY STRUGGLES

Easy Being Green was conceived as a straight business response to an emerging consumer interest, making homes more environmentally sustainable. It's fair to say that its goals were heavily aligned with the broad goals of the government at both state and federal level. However, neither level of government, at this point, was backing up its stated environmental goals with legislation. With hindsight, it is obvious to me now that I should have explored in more detail the role of government in helping to establish a market built around reducing carbon emissions. At this point, though, I believed that the fact that a significant number of people wanted to reduce their carbon footprint was enough to create a consumer base big enough to support a business such as ours. It seemed that it was only the failure of the market that was preventing people from taking action. If I could provide a market mechanism to help them, surely it would deliver a very healthy business and a great environmental outcome.

My idea was a simple one. We would provide a retrofitting service to help people make their homes more energy efficient and environmentally sustainable. We would assess each household's current energy efficiency and suggest ways to improve it. We could also implement the necessary measures, whether by installing big items like insulation, solar panels and solar hot-water systems or by supplying less expensive items such as compact fluorescent light bulbs, blinds and curtains. We guaranteed that householders would recoup any financial outlay within ten years through reduced energy costs.

I was not alone in the belief that this was an idea whose time had come. A year after launching the business, because of low sales we had to sell a second round of shares to stay afloat. We approached one of Australia's biggest banks, ANZ, with a joint project based on a survey it had commissioned which showed that 20 per cent of their customers would take up an easy service delivery option for making their house more environmentally friendly if it was offered. The ANZ bank has one-fifth of the total banking market in Australia, so the size of that market opportunity was quite substantial. I raised more funds to build the capacity of the company so as to make an offer to 20 per cent of the bank's customers.

What was fascinating was that although individuals, when asked, said they would take the opportunity to make their homes more environmentally sustainable, in the four months we trialled making the offering—and we made it to tens of thousands—only a handful of customers came forward. I thought long and hard about why this was the case. Why did people profess a willingness to spend money to make their homes more environmentally efficient, but then fail to follow through when the opportunity was offered to them? One reason, I think, is that although in our hearts we are committed to making environmental change, once you ask someone to spend money on a particular thing they begin to consider their other options for spending that money. Even though we could demonstrate that improving their home's energy efficiency would save them money in the medium term, this was less tangible than the benefits of, say, a new car, a holiday, school fees or a home renovation.

This was true even with lower-cost items like energy-efficient light bulbs. While people clearly accept it is important to make these changes, fewer than 5 per cent of people in developed countries have changed their light bulbs without being offered massive incentives to do so. Every time you replace a conventional light bulb with an energy-efficient one, you save the money you spent on it in less than a year, and many such bulbs will last five, ten or even fifteen years. It makes perfect sense financially; however, sense is not enough. At the moment, when they're shopping for a light bulb and there's one for 50p or 50c versus one for £3 or $3, most people tend to consider the outlay rather than the ongoing savings.

We'd spent two years trying to develop a market response to a perceived consumer demand and we were now faced with the very real possibility of going out of business. At this stage most of our work had been done in the state of Victoria, but we had the opportunity of doing some work for Greenpeace in New South Wales. As part of that work, we came across the NSW Greenhouse Abatement Scheme, which was created as a result of some great government legislation.

THE NEXT STAGE

The NSW state government had created a target for energy retailers to create energy efficiency or reduce their sales by 3 per cent a year. If they did not meet the target they would be fined about $16 for every tonne of carbon dioxide their lack of energy efficiency created. This effectively put a value on carbon emissions reduction. The government recognised that energy retailers might have difficulty in meeting the target, so it established a system whereby other organisations could become accredited to deliver emissions savings, which they could sell on to the energy retailers. Because the fine was set at $16 a tonne, the price was likely to oscillate somewhere below that figure. In fact, in a year of our trading in that market, the price fluctuated between $11 and $14 most of the time. That scheme was established by a state government that recognised the short-sightedness of the federal government in refusing to ratify the Kyoto Protocol and therefore deciding to create its own mini Kyoto compliance scheme. The Greenhouse Abatement

Scheme, set up in a state of around seven million people, became the second-largest carbon trading system in the world; only the Kyoto Protocol was larger.

We became aware that under the scheme a few companies, including an energy retailer, were giving away energy-efficient light bulbs. In exchange for the bulbs people were asked to assign the carbon savings thus generated to the company. The companies giving away those bulbs were then able to trade these savings to energy retailers. We explored this idea over a few months, and by the end of 2005 we had started to operate in NSW. Initially we set up stalls at weekend open-air markets, but we quickly learned that there was a real possibility of our distributing light bulbs to the whole population of the state. The trouble was that it had taken me two years to work that out; now I was rapidly running out of both money and energy. I was also operating from Victoria with an idea that only worked in NSW because of the state legislation there.

It was about this time that I met up with Paul Gilding, whom I had known at my time at the Brotherhood of St Laurence and who was a former CEO of Greenpeace both in Australia and then internationally. For ten years he had been working with businesses to incorporate sustainability into their value base. Paul instantly understood the business model I was trying to develop. More importantly, he understood where I was coming from as a social entrepreneur, and what we might be on the cusp of achieving.

Paul and I got on very well and quickly decided to work together. In addition to his confidence, which boosted my spirits after two years of struggling to build a successful business, he also brought the business some much needed capital. More importantly, the partnership brought an office, staff and connections in the NSW government.

While the company had had some success, we now had a base in NSW that allowed us to explore ways of delivering energy efficiency to tens of thousands of households.

At the start of 2006 we were a small player in the field of greenhouse abatement, with most of the work being done by two other businesses, Fieldforce and Neco, as well as the domestic power provider Origin Energy. But there were also others entering the market. By August that year, EBG had offered free light bulbs to 250,000 households out of 2 million in the entire state. The scheme was coming to an end because we, along with other businesses, had worked out how to deliver our service quickly and efficiently to large numbers of consumers. In the last month of the scheme, September 2006, we reached another 250,000 households. In total, 70 per cent of homes in NSW received their free pack of light bulbs and AAA rated shower head. It was at this point that the government adjusted the rules of the scheme to make it less financially rewarding to give away the products. I had no quarrel with this, as demand had largely been met, but it meant that phase of our business had come to an end.

What we had learnt, however, was that good government legislation could help create a market for the value it wanted to achieve—in this case, reducing carbon emissions. It also allowed enterprises to enter that market. In the case of our company, we had been able to reach 20 per cent of the market within a month; over a period of six months we, with our competitors, had reached 60 per cent of the market. In that six months we had distributed 3.5 million light bulbs to just over half a million households; we had reduced carbon emissions by 3.2 million tonnes; we were also saving 6 gigalitres of water a year because we had included a low-flow shower head with each pack of light bulbs.

Under the rules of the scheme companies were able to claim only 80 per cent of light bulbs distributed. We also had to follow up on the households that had accepted the products to ensure they had been installed within twelve months. Our research showed that more than 80 per cent of the light bulbs we had distributed were installed, results that were verified by an external auditor. That year our business had a turnover of close to $40 million, with around 20 per cent net profit on that activity.

Suddenly we had found a way of massively reducing carbon emissions in a way that was attractive to consumers; it reduced their energy bills by between $100 and $200 a year, and we were giving them $100 worth of product free of charge. We'd had them queuing in the aisles to get the product, which is why we were able to get to tens of thousands of people a week by the time we had finished the program.

The NSW government attained its goal at no cost because it was being paid for by the energy retailers, yet it brought significant reductions in carbon emissions and increased water savings. The energy providers, on average, reduced the cost of their fines from around $16 a tonne of carbon to $12 a tonne, the average price during the time that we were trading. Consumers received new, quality products in their homes that saved them money and also allowed them to feel good about their green commitment. We had been able to bring those three things together and deliver great jobs for young people as well as generating significant and healthy profits. This added up to a vibrant market that encouraged competition, job creation and innovation. Social enterprise and value-centred market economics were beginning to work for Easy Being Green.

EMERGING ISSUES

Our success also created some significant issues for us as an organisation. The project that had brought Paul and me, and our respective businesses, together was now changing. We had been very successful—we had ended up the market leader as a distributor of energy-efficiency products. While the project was moving, Paul and the team in NSW had focused on the delivery and the roll-out, and I had been building a team in Victoria that was looking at other options for the business. When the Greenhouse Abatements Scheme changed, some differences began to emerge between Paul and me. These resulted in his buying me out and my creating a new business called Cool **nrg**.

While both Paul and I were committed to the same goal—the reduction of carbon emissions—we had different styles of delivering it. Paul's was a more classical corporate or managerial approach, focusing on the key performance indicators of the business and managing it accordingly. My focus is more on teamwork and trusting the team to deliver. My role, as I see it, is to lead the team and to create and discover opportunities for the business. In the time of uncertainty as we came to the end of our project in NSW, those differences became more difficult to reconcile. For Paul, it was important to focus on more tangible options such as the exploration of a slightly tougher, but nevertheless continuing business in NSW under a regulated trading system. I believed this approach was too risky and did not build on what we had learnt.

For me, it was vital to build on our experience in NSW to launch a global business in line with my original intention, and to diversify into some other areas such as voluntary carbon trading and other energy-efficient products. If this had been our only difference, I'm sure our partnership could have continued, but it wasn't.

We also differed on the issue of our share ownership. Because of my desire to build a business culture focused on the people who made up the team, Easy Being Green had numerous shareholders, including many of the staff. I owned 50 per cent of the company, with the other 50 per cent owned by my friends and colleagues. Before combining our businesses, Paul owned 90 per cent of his business, Ecos, with one other shareholder owning the remaining 10 per cent. When we brought the two businesses together to form the new Easy Being Green, I owned 25 per cent of that company, while Paul owned 45 per cent. This set-up worked well while we were concentrating our energies on operating within the NSW Greenhouse Abatement Scheme. However, once that avenue was less important to us, I believed that the focus of our operations should be the international opportunities that were opening up. I saw that my role was to lead that international development and the research of products for that development.

In addition, I wanted to create the opportunity for more staff to have a stake in the business and also even up the benefits that Paul and I would draw from its success. I wanted him to reduce his shareholding to allow the inclusion of others as shareholders. From my perspective it appeared that Paul had no problem with that idea. Understandably, though, he was reluctant to be the one who sacrificed the most financially to achieve it.

For me, if I was going to lead the company in its international focus, it was important to restructure the business so as to include more of the staff as stakeholders and for Paul and I to have equal ownership. Again, I don't think this issue alone was enough to bring us to splitting the business;

there were ways I believe we could have resolved it. It was our third area of difference that made it clear to me that either I would have to buy Paul out or vice versa. That area of difference was the degree of financial risk we were each prepared to take.

TIME TO GO GLOBAL

At the end of January 2007, I returned to Australia after attending the World Economic Forum. I had been mulling over the idea of developing an international business, whose form I had been discussing and testing with people at the WEF. As I noted in the previous chapter, I recognised that there was a huge willingness now among people around the world to act on global warming, but little leadership in the area. Very few projects had been started with that end and none that would push forward quickly enough to achieve the change that was almost universally believed to be urgent and essential.

My experience with the NSW Greenhouse Abatement Scheme had shown me that it was relatively simple to change most of the light bulbs and shower heads in a particular region in just a few weeks. In 2006, our small company created 1 per cent of global carbon credits. That one simple initiative could be achieved in every country in the world, with the potential to save tens of millions of tonnes of carbon emissions. Given that the products were available and many nations had a legislative framework or were developing one, I thought my leadership contribution right now should be to push for such action globally. I came back to Australia determined to convince Paul that EBG should open offices in the UK and the US.

Once again our differing business styles came into play. I was responding not to an existing framework or a proven market, but to what I believed I could make happen. My role as an entrepreneur, as I saw it, was to take advantage of the current nexus: the emerging development of energy-efficient products and the desire of governments and people to act on global warming. That opportunity was here now, and although there were few significant carbon trading schemes my gut feeling was that we could take advantage of the desire for change that was building around the world.

I was not able to convince Paul; basically we had a difference on the level of risk we were willing to take with the business. I was ready to back myself and what I saw as possible; he was more committed to building on what we had already achieved in a known environment. Ironically, I believed that remaining in the NSW market was a bigger risk than the alternative. I realised that I had come together with Paul to further my commitment to the ten people I had started with three years before: to build a global business to respond to global environmental issues with initiatives that we would export from Australia. I felt that if I didn't continue moving forward, I would no longer be living out that commitment.

COOL NRG

Within a couple of weeks of my return from the WEF, and with remarkably little angst but with a lot of care for each other and from people in both organisations, we were able to redefine the business. I sold my stake to Paul's company, Ecos, leaving him the major shareholder. Sadly, before the year was out, Easy Being Green almost went into liquidation, unable to survive in the changed NSW framework for greenhouse abatement and with no other significant revenue stream. The company was eventually sold by the administrator to the power company Jackgreen, which wanted the brand to improve its green credentials. A sad misappropriation of our VCME approach.

We reached the decision to split the business on a Wednesday, and I spent that night with a friend and colleague literally weeping over the loss. Just a few days earlier, I had overheard my son Charlie telling his sister Holly that they would take over Easy Being Green one day. How would I explain the loss of my business to Charlie?

I was also apprehensive about what it would mean for all the friends and family members who had backed me in the enterprise, and for my work colleagues. I was surprised by my emotional reaction and the amount of crying I did. I'd been a human billboard for the last couple of years, wearing a company T shirt at the World Economic Forum, at meetings with political and economic leaders around the world. All of a sudden the little brand that I had put so much of my life into creating was no longer mine.

The next day, Thursday, I woke up with the realisation that I could now move ahead with my global commitment to a global business with an impact. I knew I would create an international business, and although I slipped back now and then into tears and distress, by the end of the day I had solidified the idea for my new company, got some friends and colleagues enthused about it, and secured commitments for almost $A2 million. A large portion of the finances was secured due to the leap of faith that Paul Ostling, then COO of Ernst and Young Global, was prepared to make in the new venture. My new company, as yet unnamed, was already valued at $5 million.

Standing at the threshold of my new business, I had a clear idea of what I had to offer. First, I knew through my work with Easy Being Green in NSW that it was possible to conduct a mass energy-efficiency campaign that not only reduced carbon emissions but also significantly boosted community awareness of the issue. Second, through my experience in Victoria—where we had successfully lobbied, consulted and supported the state government to the point where it had set up a greenhouse-gas abatement scheme—I knew I had the skills and knowledge to achieve the same outcome elsewhere.

I wanted to use the lessons we had learned from that process, along with my experience with the NSW scheme, to create an international market and respond to it. With those lessons, suddenly every state and country in Europe and every state in the US was a potential market. We knew how to quickly improve energy efficiency on a large scale and how to convince governments to support such a drive or face the catastrophic effect of not doing so. At the time of writing, that's exactly the enterprise I have now embarked on.

By Friday we'd come up with a name: Cool **nrg**; I'd met with the staff from the Melbourne office, most of whom had committed to continue working with me and help launch the new business. So by Day 2 we had a company name, a core idea for the business, $2 million, some great shareholders and a great global opportunity.

At the first Cool **nrg** staff meeting, the agenda was to sort out how we would establish the business. I began by offering the team 20 per cent of the business as an employee fund. The next day, because of the share sales, each individual share in that employee fund was valued at $100,000. So, right from the start, we were beginning to share both ownership and leadership of the company in the way that I wanted.

By the end of the following week, we'd taken on a couple of new employees and developed a strategy that included going to the US and Britain. There was the potential for some Clean Development Mechanism (CDM) projects (this is the mechanism within the Kyoto Protocol that allows European countries to fund energy efficiency in developing countries as a way of meeting their Kyoto commitments) that meant that we would also look at moving rapidly into Singapore, Thailand and India.

By the second week we'd put together an extraordinarily committed team. One of my colleagues had left for London to set up an office there, another had gone to San Francisco to do the same, and two others were in India, looking at setting up a project whereby a million female community workers would sell energy-efficient light bulbs to fund their activities.

Almost three years to the day after I'd left the Brotherhood of St Laurence, I was realising my goal of establishing a business that responded to a pressing social and environmental issue and was connected to the country I lived in. It was going to have a new name: Cool **nrg**.

THE FUTURE

Beginning in the summer of 2006–07, Australia experienced its driest twelve months on record. The demand for water tanks in urban areas is so great that suppliers are having difficulty in meeting it. The federal government announced in February 2007 that it would establish a cap-and-trade emissions trading system by 2011 and phase out incandescent light bulbs, a move that looks likely to be replicated around the world.

Is a carbon trading scheme supported by government legislation necessary, given that consumers already seem to be moving towards products and services that are more environmentally sustainable? At this point, after some success as a provider of those goods and services, I am now more convinced than ever that the majority of people won't act on the environment unless such action on mandatory carbon emissions reduction is made extremely financially attractive.

> Social entrepreneurship should actually be called entrepreneurship for social innovation. This means that the ingredients for entrepreneurship—like creativity, courage, perseverance—have to be applied in order to bring about social change. The social mission is the important thing, whether it is achieved by a for-profit or a not-for-profit activity.
>
> *Hilde Schwab, President and Co-Founder, Schwab Foundation for Social Entrepreneurship*

Demand for energy-efficient and water-saving products has increased massively. However, these are still marginal products in terms of the mass market. And even then, people in general aren't buying water tanks for altruistic reasons; it's because they want to be able to continue to water their gardens, wash their cars and fill their swimming pools—things they are prevented from doing because of current water restrictions due to drought. Ultimately, self-interest supports their environmental commitment rather than the reverse. This is not to say that their commitment isn't real, but that only when people feel the impact of their actions, or non-actions, in a real and immediate way do they change their habits.

It isn't my role to judge people on the how and why of their decision making or to be negative about it, but simply to recognise the reality of a situation and develop a solution that works within that reality. If that solution is relatively easy to adopt, makes financial sense and makes people feel proud that they are doing the right thing (as well as saving the planet)—so much the better for all of us. I think that's social enterprise. Sadly, what it says about value-centred market economics is that the market will only have those social values in it if governments lead that market and give it a purpose and a framework. Otherwise we'll continue to buy our gas-guzzling cars, drain the water from our rivers until they're dry, and stuff ourselves with fast food.

8

Cool nrg: The internals of a social-purpose business

Launching Cool **nrg** in March 2007 allowed me to create another company around the core idea of greenhouse gas abatement. I felt privileged to have the opportunity of starting again with Cool **nrg**. I was able to look back and assess what had really worked and what hadn't. I was also able to consider the possibility of building a business that was completely driven by social values, yet would still thrive and be profitable.

Three key factors influenced my deliberations on the structure of Cool **nrg**. Some I considered on a conscious level, but others were more intuitive. The first was the nature of the marriage between the business and its social goal (in the case of Cool **nrg**, greenhouse gas abatement); the second was the culture of an organisation that wishes to achieve a big social or environmental goal globally; and the third was the structures needed to support a business driven by purpose rather than profit.

MARRYING BUSINESS WITH A SOCIAL PURPOSE

Social enterprise or social business is a great way to deliver social values in a market economy, and building such enterprises and exploring their nature have been my passions for the past fifteen years. The term social enterprise has been applied to a range of innovative practices and philosophies within the business, welfare and not-for-profit sectors. However, it means more than just business acting ethically or working with charities, or charities embracing business principles. For me, social enterprise is the marriage between the market and a social purpose. People buy the enterprise's product or service because it will save them money and give them something they want within the context of a market economy. This obviously means it must be comparable in terms of price to similar products or services.

For me, exploring how to deliver a social value through a business model began at Easy Being Green and then continued with Paul Gilding. He had already spent a long time thinking about the relationship between social goals and the market, and we began to use the terms 'purpose-driven organisation' and 'campaigning corporation' to describe our business. The first term implies that the business has other goals beyond profit. In some ways you could say most businesses are purpose driven; their purpose is to maximise profits. However, our purpose was not only to make money. We wanted to have an impact on climate change by helping to reduce carbon emissions. Having such a clearly defined aim was very helpful when the board and the senior management team made decisions. It allowed us to consider any question in the light of that goal as well as the imperative to remain profitable.

The need to remain profitable we took as read, because otherwise we'd go out of business. Yet it was a lower-order consideration. Generally, any decision coming to the board or to the senior management team had already been considered in light of its profitability. It had to make sense in terms of market economics, or as an investment that would create financial opportunity in the future. So the question for us was to measure those decisions against our purpose, which was always, 'Is this activity, while it may be profitable, going to help reduce global carbon emissions?'

Answering this question meant that we made some unorthodox decisions on the question of competition. We realised that competition was good for carbon abatement, as it would force us to operate as efficiently and as innovatively as possible and to look constantly for new opportunities. It also meant that other entrepreneurs, seeing that it was possible to operate a profitable business in this sector, would come into the market and also help reduce greenhouse gases. Clearly, one company alone cannot solve an issue like greenhouse gas abatement, where carbon emissions need to be reduced by millions of tonnes every year. Rather than making decisions that would restrict the competition we faced, we often chose to support the entry of others into our market space. For example, we campaigned for the creation of conditions to foster a commercial environment that would encourage competition. We also chose higher-quality, less profitable products, because we wanted consumers to have a good experience with us. This, we hoped, would encourage them to consider purchasing other energy-efficient products in the future. It was because we were a purpose-driven business that we were able to make these types of decisions.

The other phrase that we frequently used to describe the company was 'campaigning corporation'. It was a term coined by Paul and initially I resisted it, but by the time I started Cool **nrg** it was the term I preferred. It conveys the idea of a business that is both designed to generate wealth, be financially responsible and wants to bring social values into the market. Because we were driven by the goal of reducing the impact of climate change, we strove to work with governments, institutions, other businesses and the not-for-profit sector to create the opportunities to allow us to succeed. In an organisation driven solely by profit, this is called lobbying, not campaigning. The difference is that lobbying implies self-interest. In the case of Easy Being Green and now Cool **nrg**, which I would also consider a campaigning corporation, we're campaigning for a market that will accommodate many businesses, all delivering products and services that reduce carbon emissions.

All this talk of lobbying versus campaigning, and purpose-driven rather than profit-driven, could be seen as merely semantics. The multinational giant General Electric has an initiative called ecoimagination through which it strives to develop environmentally innovative technology and products. I'm sure the people who lead ecoimagination see their role within GE as being to ensure that more products come onto the market that benefit the environment. And that is right; that is their purpose. But that purpose is subjugated to the performance of GE on the stock exchange; to its return on investment or earnings per share.

By contrast, for Cool **nrg**, profit is always a by-product of a clear, purpose-driven decision. With Cool **nrg**, the company is set up in a way that its stakeholders understand that equation while recognising that it's important for us to remain profitable. The driver for each person within Cool **nrg** is the delivery of greenhouse gas abatement to a mainstream market.

> Certain things when shared are not divided but multiplied. You can say that of love, of compassion, of hope . . . As you can see, it's a very simple way of explaining feelings or actions that create a virtuous circle.
>
> Social entrepreneurship follows the same principle— namely that society as a whole wins much more when a business is coupled with a social concern. It's about common sense: how can I have a good quality of life if those surrounding me are constantly striving for food, shelter, water? I may have a haven in my house, but the moment I walk in the streets, I will be in an environment of poverty and violence.
>
> Social entrepreneurs are thus people who strive to pass on the idea that a person's well-being is dependent on the well-being of others.
>
> *Paulo Coelho is a best-selling author and board member of the Schwab Foundation for Social Entrepreneurship*

CULTURE OF A SOCIAL-PURPOSE BUSINESS OR CAMPAIGNING CORPORATION

What are the attributes of an organisation that operates as a business while simultaneously creating the very conditions and framework it operates within? Obviously a sense of vision is essential, not only to see the opportunity in an area previously owned and managed by the not-for-profit sector, but also to understand how that opportunity can be converted into a new market. This is where entrepreneurial skills come into play—the ability to deliver values-driven goals in a market-driven way.

Optimism is also crucial; you have to believe that it is possible for the market to deliver change on a vast scale. At Cool **nrg** we believe that in the next few years we will be part of a movement to replace every incandescent light bulb on the planet with an energy-efficient one. This single, admittedly massive, initiative will reduce carbon emissions by more than 5 per cent globally, a target that is almost unimaginable in that short time frame at the moment. It's almost a case of suspending one's disbelief that such bold aims are achievable. You have to be willing to see the big picture and have conversations about profound change with the political and business leaders who can make these changes happen.

A certain relentlessness is required to maintain that vision, though. Time and again, as I have promoted the initiative of replacing light bulbs, I have come across the same bureaucratic response: 'It's not possible.' While bureaucrats usually accept that such a scheme would have an immediate and far-reaching impact on carbon emissions, they stumble when confronted with the scope of such a project. Faced with such resistance, I steel myself to continue to push, persuade, demand and cajole in order to secure the outcome I so passionately believe in.

While Cool **nrg** has to remain relentless in pushing for its objective, it also has to be flexible. The carbon-emissions abatement sphere is rapidly changing and requires participants to be adaptive so as to overcome the reservations, the doubt and the concerns we encounter.

Again and again, we have to see the issue through other people's eyes and have the empathy to listen to, and the creativity to deal with, their concerns. We've had to make an argument for doing something that may not, at first glance, capture the imagination. We're not talking about replanting rainforest or ramming whaling ships but about changing light bulbs, yet that prosaic-sounding vision could have a more far-reaching and dramatic impact on the environment than many more dramatic gestures. To get up every day and be passionate about changing every light bulb in the world requires commitment to the vision and boldness in executing it. We are used to seeing this passion and vision for what might be in NGOs and other not-for-profit organisations, but not in commercial enterprises. Yet having such passionate purpose behind a business can be very useful.

At Cool **nrg**, we have built a culture where mistakes are seen as lessons learned and thus as contributions to the ultimate success of our enterprise. When it began, Cool **nrg** had sufficient financial resources to enable it to trade for a year. To me, this was perfectly acceptable, because if we hadn't achieved our goal of carbon-emissions abatement in a year then we wouldn't have been operating at the speed required to deal with the problem. As a team, we were prepared for the possibility of failing and having to look for another job. Yet professionally, we were prepared to put ourselves on the line for that twelve months, hoping success would come and we would be able to keep doing something that we passionately believed in.

That passion has paid off. Ten months after the launch of Cool **nrg** we had opened offices in Europe, Mexico, China and the US and had signed contracts to deliver two major energy efficiency projects—one in Australia and the other in the UK—using compact fluorescent light bulbs. The UK project was the largest program of its kind in the world and saw the distribution of 5 million light bulbs in one day. Funded by Scottish and Southern Energy, the light bulbs were delivered with the *Sun*, Europe's most widely read newspaper. Our future plans for the company involve the distribution of 200 million light bulbs in 2008, employing partnerships that span several countries and various companies using different funding regimes. The energy saved by the distribution and fitting of that number of light bulbs is equivalent to that supplied by ten nuclear power stations over ten years. Fifteen people in less than a year have created and delivered this possibility.

Our passion also leads directly to our willingness to take risks both personally and as a company. The deals we are putting together in other countries may mean making decisions worth hundreds of millions of dollars over a single weekend. Obviously failure on that scale would unfold very publicly. Such huge undertakings also require openness and honesty with global partners, whose support we will need because of the size of these projects. These will be people and organisations who understand our goal and who are willing to embrace our vision, and to engage with them requires open and direct communication.

The attributes of such an organisational culture as I've described make a formidable list and include, in no particular order: vision, optimism, boldness, relentlessness, flexibility, empathy, creativity, adaptability, passion, openness and a willingness to take risks. Daunting it may be, but I believe such a culture will ensure that Cool **nrg** succeeds as a purpose-driven, campaigning corporation.

I think social entrepreneurs are first and foremost practical people; people who are confronted with difficulties and try to come up with bold and innovative ideas. The fact that they have to be accountable for their actions and think inside a business framework gives a real scope to their actions: they are not merely 'giving a hand' but building something more concrete and everlasting in society. This practical concern, in my view, is the very proof of their commitment to enhance the standards of living of people who otherwise are alienated from our fast-paced world. They are in a way 'alchemists' who bring to the physical realm dreams and hopes that otherwise would seem to be unattainable.

Paulo Coelho

ELEMENTS OF A SOCIAL-PURPOSE BUSINESS

When I was designing the model for Cool **nrg** I found it useful to think about the processes and structures of a social-purpose business under the following four topics: the people within the organisation; the leadership of the organisation; how the leadership and the wider team work together; and the ownership model of such a business.

People

The Cool **nrg** team is diverse in terms of personalities and skills, yet we share some common traits. We tend to be people who have had success in our working lives, from the seventeen year old who's just joined us in administration right up to the people who are heading projects in the UK and the US. We're people who work hard, take a high level of personal responsibility and are adaptable to changing circumstances. For a business like ours, which wants to move and deliver on our goals as quickly as possible and with the inherent risks I've mentioned, the ability to accept and deal with change is a prerequisite. The people making up the team must feel secure enough to have their job description change rapidly and regularly and be prepared to look for another job in a year's time. They must also be prepared to work with a range of agencies in different countries that have committed to changing all their light bulbs.

As a group we are ambitious; ambitious to do well individually and to contribute, but also to achieve significant and profound action on climate change. Because of the work that we're doing, because of that purpose, we are willing to increase the amount of risk that we'll take on.

Our work is very much aligned with who we are as people, and this means we have a much greyer boundary between work and home. Within weeks of the company's launch, a couple of us were working overseas. Our team was spread over three different time zones around the world; we are speaking to each other simultaneously at night, early in the morning, in the middle of the night. We also mix as a community: we play together and celebrate together. We are willing to bring our home lives to work with us, sometimes literally when kids aren't well or there are problems with friends or family. I think that as a group we are glad we can bring our whole self to work—our passions, our sadnesses, our fears and our excitement.

This fluidity and vibrancy has created a community of people who can use their skills well together, who fit together in terms of their personalities, and who are also willing to tell the truth. We're able to say some things that in other organisations may be hard or impossible to say because there's a purpose that holds us together and it requires that we know what's happening with each other. Work is a place where feedback is given and received with extraordinary generosity.

There is a sense of relief, I think, when you're allowed to bring your whole self to your work, and balance your financial, social and community needs. Using your skills and talents to achieve specific social-purpose goals makes life very meaningful.

Leadership

After the people who make up the team, the next most important thing is the leadership that supports them. As leader of Cool **nrg**, I find this the most interesting part: how do I create the conditions that allow the organisation to operate in the way that I would like? When we reviewed this as a team, there was agreement that the leader's role included: having a strong vision of the organisation's goal; locating opportunities for the enterprise; and having the charisma to carry out the organisation's role, internally and externally.

A crucial part of the leadership role in an organisation like Cool **nrg** is to maintain the culture of optimism and belief in the possibility of attaining our goal. Humanity as a whole needs to get better at dreaming bigger visions and accepting the challenge of delivering on them. So certainly part of my leadership is about having the stamina to keep pushing forward. At Cool **nrg**, there is no hierarchy; instead we have a very clear delegation of responsibility. In any conversation we have about a particular task or project, we identify the person with the skills or the greatest opportunity to learn from leading or taking on a given task. And

that person may be Laura, the seventeen-year-old administrator, or it might be me or one of the directors. At Cool
nrg, while I do lead the team, we are getting much better at
recognising that anyone can lead as long as they have the
skills and the desire, and then responding to that leadership.

With such a non-hierarchical approach, it is imperative
that each of us take responsibility for the tasks we put our
hand up for. Blaming others in the team or trying to offload
responsibility once it's taken on is just not something that
we do. At the same time, everyone is encouraged to ask for
support or help if they need it.

From my perspective, being a leader in Cool **nrg** has
enabled me to thrive because it allows me to do what I do
best: having and holding on to a vision; utilising the
connections I've made in other leadership roles I've held
over the past ten years; being the entrepreneur within the
organisation; spending time with each member of the team
as they make sense of the conditions and circumstances of
the country they find themselves working in; and helping
them discover how purpose and market are going to come
together to allow our business to support a great outcome
on mitigating global warming.

With fifteen people we have fifteen styles of working,
and when someone's leading they're leading from their
style. We have an open-plan office with no partitions; often
there'll be music playing and people chatting. Sometimes
we have a barbecue lunch, sometimes everyone goes their
own way and sometimes we all go to a café. The style
changes; there's no right way. We have fifteen people who
work differently and yet well together: fast, adaptively,
supportively, having a laugh, and caring for each other.
Most importantly we are doing something that we believe
can make a really significant contribution.

In addressing social and economic challenges, all sectors of society should focus on creating a special type of value: social value. From this principle all relations tying up governments, businesses and social entrepreneurs should follow.

There's an inertia linked to governments and their institutions that explains why sometimes certain communities are left behind and their voices unheard. These are the scenarios where social entrepreneurs take the lead. They can, since they are individuals or small structures, adapt themselves and find new solutions.

Recently I read about Dina Abdel Wahab, who founded the Baby Academy for children with Down syndrome in Egypt. She says something I couldn't agree with more about the social entrepreneur's role in society, namely that: 'It is easier for me as an entrepreneur to take the risk and do something, than for the government to do that on a mass scale.'

Yet the actions of these social entrepreneurs shouldn't pass unnoticed by governments. On the contrary, governments should create a favourable environment for businesses that have social awareness in their top agenda, which can be reached through fiscal initiatives, grants, etc.

If governments actively back up social enterprises, it seems to me that the legislation would make it very difficult for traditional businesses to strive with no concern for the communities they are part of. In the same way that the social entrepreneurs take on the business framework, I think it is time for traditional businesses to take on a social framework. This can only be achieved through vigilant governments.

Paulo Coelho

Structure and responsibility

When you have a group of people working in the way I've described, all taking responsibility, inevitably you have a very non-hierarchical structure. I have little to say on this other than that we have processes and procedures made for every task but that don't necessarily fit into an overarching organisational structure.

To outside observers this may appear a chaotic and unwieldy way of working, but there is an order to it. Geoff Mulgan, the head of the Performance and Innovation Unit in Britain's Blair government, whom I mentioned in an earlier chapter, coined the term 'chaordic': combining chaos and order. It's a very useful concept for us: we allow ourselves to be creative, chaotic, changeable, but we know that to achieve our goals we must bring order, process and substance, and have clear benchmarks against which we constantly measure our success. Such a method takes hard personal development, and I have to be in a position where I can have conversations with my colleagues that are truthful, open and creative and that include honest feedback about all our efforts. Sometimes it's difficult, but it's also incredibly rewarding and supports communities, friendships and the kind of functional unit that allows each of us to bring our whole self to work.

Ownership

The last piece of what holds Cool **nrg** together is ownership. Ownership is tricky, because if the company is owned by people who are merely investing in the enterprise, it is very easy for the goal of ensuring a return on investment to become the major driver of the organisation. As an individual, I have avoided building personal wealth for the past twenty years because of my passion for the values that my contribution might bring, not the profit it might create. I own 60 per cent of Cool **nrg**. A further 40 per cent is owned by investors—almost all of them members of the organisation, whether staff or directors. Twenty per cent of pre-tax profit is shared equally between the employees. As a result, the company makes decisions non-hierarchically and collectively. There's no separation between the board and staff; the people on the board are part of the staff. We don't have a situation where somebody has a conversation with me and I have a conversation with somebody else and then I report that back; all of the people making decisions have a significant stake in the organisation.

Because I have the largest financial stake in the business I have the final say if, as a company, we are nervous about a particular risk we are taking or if we are having difficulty making a decision. Ultimately I will make that call if we can't make it collectively. It's early days as far as Cool **nrg** is concerned, and we have not reached that point to date. I actually doubt that we ever will, yet it's crucial that I have that option. This may seem a contradictory position given what I've written earlier on the non-hierarchical structure of Cool **nrg** and our sharing of responsibility. Yet my experience in Easy Being Green, and before that in the not-for-profit sector, provided me with two reasons for wanting to reserve the right to make final decisions on particular issues if necessary. The first is that once there is a perceived obligation to produce a financial return on an investment it is very easy for that objective to become the primary one. The second is that time and time again, I have seen how decision making can get bogged down in discussions about process. I want to ensure that our team is not distracted by the process but can focus on the outcome.

I see this as providing a necessary circuit breaker rather than being controlling or heavy-handed. Effectively it gives me, in any discussion, chairman status. I am able to draw conversations and discussions to a conclusion so a decision can be made then and there, not in a week's time after consultations with the board.

Operating a for-profit business in the area of social change is not without its dilemmas, particularly for someone like me who hasn't had personal wealth as a life goal. Sometimes I am asked, 'But what will you do with all the money, Nic, if the business does incredibly well?' It's as if the purpose that drives Cool **nrg** will be tainted in some way by financial success. Frankly, it's a question I hope to have to wrestle with because it will mean that we are achieving our goal of carbon emissions abatement within the mechanism we have chosen—the market. It is important for purpose-driven organisations to go up against others in the marketplace to deliver environmental and social outcomes alongside their profit-driven enterprises, and I want to win in that fight.

9

The end of charity

When I first started thinking about this book, it had the working title 'For Love or Money'. I wanted the title to capture the dichotomy at the heart of the cycle of separateness I talked about in the first chapter. This cycle divorces business from social value, and charity and the welfare sector from financially sustainable practices.

I've tried to capture a similar concept with the phrase value-centred market economics. This refers to the theory of viewing the market as a tool for delivering a range of values besides just profit. It's an attempt to bring together two seemingly diametrically opposed concepts. One is social values like concern for our neighbours and for the world and the other is the more hard-edged notion of the marketplace and the goods and services it makes available to us. I've expressed it very simply here, but putting it into practice is complicated. It requires choosing among a myriad of options to find the best way to deliver not just material goods and economic wealth, but things like high-quality, accessible health care and education; affordable housing; a cohesive and compassionate society; a robust and vibrant democracy; and a sustainable and cared-for environment. By embedding these 'soft' concepts in the market, I hope to encourage new and innovative ways of thinking about the economy and the ways it can be manipulated for the benefit of all.

Externalities is an economic term that refers to factors that, while they may not have a direct cost to business, do impose costs on the wider society. These externalities, or broader values, are generally recognised by businesses or market models only when it is forced upon them. This is achieved most effectively through legislation that gives externalities a direct cost to businesses and so creates a level playing field for competition. For example, renewable sources of energy will thrive, and replace coal, once the true price of carbon pollution is added to every tonne of coal burned. It may be that value-centred market economics doesn't perfectly capture the concept of the market as something that encompasses more than just trade, profit and loss, but I do believe that to work in different ways we must first give those new ways of working a name.

Social enterprise and social-purpose business are interchangeable terms that already have currency. They refer to market-based activity that aims to deliver broader social values. My company, Cool **nrg**, is a for-profit social enterprise. If the business thrives, it will have a radical impact on global carbon emissions; however, my colleagues and I will have to be as enterprising and shrewd as the very best businesspeople if we are to succeed. We struggle with the real prospects of both failure and financial success. As I write, both outcomes appear equally possible. Social entrepreneurship doesn't guarantee success, but it makes doing business much more honourable and enjoyable. I hope that the complexity I've been talking about becomes more embedded in all the various sectors—welfare, business, government—so that they all shift closer to value-centred market economics.

The social entrepreneur is the actor or agent; he or she begins with the desire to use the market to deliver social values, and then employs the market to deliver those values. I am that person at Cool **nrg** although there are now others within the business with these skills. Being an entrepreneur is never simple and is always a roller-coaster ride. Doing it in a sustainable way that means caring for—even loving—those you work with and serve can make for an exhilarating ride, but it is also an extraordinary privilege.

I've also used the term spirited sustainability to describe the style of leadership needed to work in this different way. Once you step out of the world of charity and embrace the market, you immediately challenge those who remain wedded to the traditional view of the various sectors and the way they should operate. I've been accused of selling out, of abandoning my values to line my pockets. Those accusations have hurt. In fact, I am risking everything I have to make a difference on a problem that I believe threatens humanity. Breaking boundaries, shaking up the status quo, working in a deeper and more sustainable way takes passion and spirit, and a bit of missionary zeal. This is what I mean when I talk about spirited sustainability. It's what you need as a social entrepreneur to push through old boundaries in order to move from the simplicity of a dollar-based market to a more complex market that embraces social goals as well. It's a quality of leadership that has passion, love and persistence at its core.

What I also wanted to capture with the term value-centred market economics was the idea that the market can be part of the solution. Although the market is an entrenched part of many social problems, it is the system we've got and we have to work with it. There's no point, as some charities and NGOs do, trying to operate within some kind of parallel universe that does not engage with the market. Value-centred market economics and social enterprise, I believe, are our best options for finding ways we might live better within the paradigm we've got. And they can do so in a way that can lead us towards a more sustaining mix of priorities, allowing us to take better care of the planet and each other. As I wrote in an earlier chapter the market is a tool, and one we can learn to wield much more skilfully. The market is only the problem while it is linked solely to monetary values. There also has to be some mechanism for ordering externalities, whether they be care for the environment or care for each other. And the market can fulfil that role, but only if we decide to use it that way.

I was encouraged in December 2006 by the maiden speech of Evan Thornley to the Victorian Parliament. Evan is a former student union leader, the entrepreneur behind the immensely successful Internet company LookSmart, and now a state Labor parliamentarian. I include some excerpts from one of his speeches here because of the insights it offers into the role of government and the social uses of the market.

Some believe politics is a contest between belief in markets and belief in the state, but since I believe in both and since I am more interested in how we can have effective markets and an effective state, I find this contest a waste of time. Our society has a certain genius about it that balances the system of one dollar, one value within a framework of one vote, one value. The proportions of the show in each sector have hardly moved a jot for a very long time. It is not the fight that matters.

Some believe politics is becoming a contest between the economy and the planet. But this misunderstands rigorous economics, which should recognise externalities and price them into the market. The fight against climate change is a chance for growth, not a reason to stop it—as the Stern report recently showed. There is no more important issue that we face, but the risk to our economy is in being the ostrich, rather than having the courage to face reality and make a virtue of the problem by grabbing first mover advantage in creating the solutions . . .

So if all these contests are for naught, you might be wondering what there is left to debate—why we cannot all just continue down some bland, centrist course to happiness. It is because, while I reject all these old contests and refuse to fight in these last wars, there remains one central contest that shows no sign of disappearing. It is the contest between the virtuous cycles and the vicious cycles of human behaviour. It is a contest between the builders— the people who understand that by investing in each other we all win—and the sharp-elbows brigade.

Members of the sharp-elbows brigade have a faulty understanding of the world. They believe that for you to have something must mean I cannot. The genius of investing in people—that by investing in people now, we can both have more later—has passed them by. And so they believe that by inflicting damage on you, I will somehow be advantaged and, perhaps even more absurdly, that you will not respond in kind and inflict damage on me. My experiences of life have taught me that the sharp-elbows brigade is wrong.

In business you learn the difference between the P and L and the balance sheet—the difference between what you get for today and what you invest for tomorrow. The purpose of government is not to take money from individuals with one hand and give the same money back to the same individuals with the other. The purpose is to pool the resources of the community to get to the scale where we can invest in the things that we all need and which bring us all future benefits.

As it turns out, the investments which generate the greatest returns, the things that can deliver the biggest future benefit are the investments in the people themselves—what the economists call human capital. A dollar invested in early-childhood development returns nine dollars. A dollar invested in preventative health care now can save many dollars in the future. A dollar spent in preventing road trauma returns many times over in reduced health care costs, welfare costs and lost productivity . . .

As for the title I ended up choosing for this book, why does the success of social business and the adoption of value-centred market economics mean the end of charity? It's because charity upholds the separation between the sectors when it claims 'doing good' as its exclusive province. We need to end the dichotomy that allows charity to claim the moral high ground by defining itself in opposition to business and vice versa. It's the other side of the equation that doesn't allow the change. This makes a circle that feeds off itself. That's why we need the end of charity, and social business can help bring that about. When charities cease to exist, it won't mean the end of good works or the end of compassion. It will just mean we have developed more efficient, holistic and sustainable ways of dealing with the issues we face. *Caritas*, the Latin word for love, and the root of the word charity, needs always to be at the heart of our existence, but let it also be at the heart of our business enterprises. Rather than confining charity to 1 per cent or 10 per cent of our activity, let's infuse all we do with it. We will all be a lot happier.

Of course some governments and organisations have long recognised and developed ways to use and manipulate the market to deliver a broad range of values. Increasingly, too, individuals are choosing how to spend their money in ways that support ethical business practices and products. By naming these activities and choices as value-centred market economics, I want to advocate that this way of thinking and acting be adopted at the very core of how all businesses, including charities, operate, and how all consumers make decisions about what they buy, save or invest in. Our ability to take more complex approaches to issues that matter to us, to our communities and to the world's peace and prosperity will benefit us all. But to do this we all need to grapple with our own unique situations while taking into account our neighbours and the planet.

Our nations desperately chase ever growing wealth, productivity and growth. The emerging giants of China and India are demonstrating that rapid growth can have a massive cost, including large-scale environmental degradation and huge disparities between those who benefit from economic growth and those who are left behind. If the global community cannot find fairer ways to share the planet's resources and our collective knowledge and experience, if we cannot place economic development in the context of a healthy environment with healthy people, we— and increasingly, those large and rapidly developing nations—will face escalating social problems. It is not enough to blame the market economy for these problems. The market is a blunt implement driven all too often by a purely financial hammer. But we can use the market to help order our time and resources and help in our decision making. We need to keep this in mind every time we buy household goods, or choose how to educate our children, where to invest our money, or what we let our children watch on TV. If we opt for the simplicity of caring only about financial values, the market will fail us, and we will fail ourselves and our communities.

As I've argued, government and business have key roles to play in moving us towards a value-centred market economy. Once government has set the agenda, public servants need to step up and accept the challenge to allow the different sectors to take their role. Rather than hindering new enterprises, the public sector must encourage flexibility and adaptability to release the procedures, the funding and the mechanisms for all sectors to use. They must accept the risk of driving change, not avoid it. Leadership and vision are essential. Our politicians and public servants have become too risk averse. Short election cycles and, in some cases, multiple tiers of government are partly to blame, but a real dynamism needs to be injected into the public sector to energise debate, encourage innovation and support initiative.

Multinational corporations' simplistic way of operating often means that they are willing to do whatever is necessary to achieve their goal of increasing profit. In the search for market share, growth, productivity and profits, many companies—right down the scale to small corner stores— choose the opportunity to generate income rather than supporting the values of either the people they serve or the countries they work in.

I hope this book will not only be read by the few of us who recognise ourselves as social entrepreneurs but by businesspeople who are interested in delivering more than a comfortable profit margin. I also hope that when they accept the value-centred challenge they will improve their companies' market share, share price and longevity. It's worked for some—Salesforce, The Body Shop, Toyota and GE, with its ecoimagination. I hope the book will be picked up by students in business schools who might be looking for a quote to include in their essay on corporate social responsibility, and end up considering how to include some value-centred ideas on productivity or wealth generation. I hope it will be read by social workers who may be disillusioned with the market system yet understand the value of marketing, of productivity, of good management practices. I hope it will be read by politicians trying to understand social entrepreneurship and that it will show them how they can create policies that allow social entrepreneurs to emerge and thrive. I hope it encourages board members of multinationals, mulling over whether they should take early retirement, to realise they could use the last years of their careers to bring to their professional lives the quality and complexity that they dream of bringing to their personal lives. I hope the book starts a discussion that will help society to move beyond the idea that 'charity' is the only place for 'good works'; or that giving 1 per cent or 0.5 per cent of our income to charity can assuage our guilt about the way we live. One per cent is not enough to change the world. We need to change ourselves and the choices we make in all areas of our lives: our home, our work, our clubs and our communities. That's a more complex way to live, but in my experience it's been the key to discovering the deepest relationships and the greatest qualities in my life.

At a personal level, I hope continuing to explore these ideas will challenge me to make better decisions for myself and my family; to make my relationships more loving; to become a better manager of the people I work with; to spend more time talking with people who are making difficult decisions about the futures of their countries.

The end of charity—it sounds bleak, doesn't it? But I'm not talking about the end of love. In fact I'm talking about the opposite. We've taken the love out of doing business. I want it back, because we spend a lot of time at work and we should be doing it with love as well as for the money.

Index

The Iremonger Award for Writing on Public Issues

Allen & Unwin is Australia's largest independent publisher, with a reputation for publishing 'books that matter'. Accordingly, Allen & Unwin is pleased to offer The Iremonger Award for Writing on Public Issues, an award for non-fiction works of political, social and cultural commentary that deal with contemporary Australian issues and contribute to public debate. On offer is prize money of $10 000, guaranteed publication, royalties on book sales and editorial support to develop the proposal into a finished manuscript.

John Iremonger's outstanding 35 year publishing career helped shape Australia's perception of its past and spotlighted the challenges of its future. He published many groundbreaking books and leading Australian writers and was integral to the establishment of Allen & Unwin's reputation as a leading Australian publisher. John also founded the independent publishing house Hale & Iremonger and was Director of Melbourne University Press. Conditions of entry and entry forms can be obtained from www.allenandunwin.com/iremongeraward